# British Columbia

## Spirit of the People

# British Columbia

## Spirit of the People

Jean Barman

**Page 1: A massive inunnguaq built atop Whistler Mountain to embody the spirit of the 2010 Olympic and Paralympic Winter Games. An inunnguaq is an inukshuk shaped like a person.** *Photo Randy Lincks*

**Pages 2–3: A snowy day in British Columbia's Cariboo country.** *Photo Vance Hanna*

**This page: British Columbia's fabulous inside waters are a boater's paradise.** *Photo Boomer Jerritt*

# Contents

# Foreword
## The First 150 Years

This year British Columbians come together to celebrate 150 years of achievements, triumphs and challenges that have shaped this great province we call home. The people and events that have created the province we live in today are unlike any other. Ours is a land of diversity that has captured the imaginations of people from every continent, who have come here for a better life. This land has produced great artists, academics, scientists, adventurers, athletes, environmentalists and all-around leaders.

This book will take you on a journey back through time, people and places—a journey that starts in 1858 when British Columbia stood suspended between two worlds: the First Nations, who had established a rich, mature culture dating back many millennia, and the Western industrial world, spearheaded by England and other European nations. The first and most transformative wave came in the form of some thirty thousand non-aboriginal miners in 1858, mostly American veterans of the California gold rush of 1849. The century and a half that followed presented both challenges and great opportunity.

**Premier Gordon Campbell speaks at the sod-turning of the Squamish-Lil'wat Cultural Centre in the village of Whistler, co-host of the 2010 Olympics.**
*Photo Bonny Makarewicz*

Our 150th anniversary gives us not only cause to reflect on our history, but a reason to look forward into our future. What will British Columbia be like ten, fifty or a hundred years from now? What can we do today to secure the future for our children and grandchildren? We live in a world redefined by enormous shifts in our demographic, economic and environmental makeup. British Columbians, brimming with optimism and confidence, have the opportunity to lead in a way that many parts of the world will follow.

From the vibrant First Nations cultures to the first European explorers to gold rush prospectors to overlanders to new immigrants arriving daily in search of a better life, British Columbia's history and future has always been one of new arrivals, evolving cultures, and changing demographics. BC's present and future is inextricably tied to the people and countries of the Pacific. Those links will strengthen over the next several decades in education, in science and technology, in culture and art and in investment and business.

Beginning with the rich history of the First Nations, each new arrival to British Columbia brings new ideas and new perspectives that further enrich our province. Our evolution has proven to be a most admirable effort, one that created a robust, egalitarian, multicultural society that faces the challenge of the new millennium with justifiable confidence and is ready to contribute even more to the global village. It is a good time to pause and take stock of where we have been, what we have learned and how we have contributed to our nation and our world. It is a time when we can move forward into the next chapter of British Columbia's history with greater understanding and renewed purpose for what we can achieve together.

Premier Gordon Campbell
*Province of British Columbia*

Opposite: **A totem pole occupies a place of honour on the grounds of the British Columbia Legislative Buildings in Victoria.**
*Photo Chris Cheadle*

Pages 6–7: **Mount Drysdale and Rockwell Pass in Kootenay National Park.**
*Photo John E. Marriott*

# 1

# The Best Place on Earth

British Columbia is not one of those places where the landscape reposes quietly in the background. Here geography impresses itself on people's affairs. It rears up, it stretches out, it is overpowering, it is serene, it is humid, it is arid, it separates and it unites. And there is really a lot of it. At 947,800 square kilometres, or about 366,000 square miles, the westernmost Canadian province is nearly as big as the American states of Texas and California combined and almost four times the size of Great Britain.

British Columbia hovers on the edge of a continent. The Pacific Ocean washing toward Asia marks the province's western boundary, mountains frame most of British Columbia on the east, the United States bounds it on the south and an inhospitable climate borders it on the north.

Previous pages: **A lone climber is reduced to a speck atop Serra II in the Waddington group. Mt. Waddington in the Coast Range is British Columbia's highest mountain.** *Photo John Baldwin*

The province's location caused it to be visited by dinosaurs 130 million years ago, but also to be one of the last areas of North America colonized by Europeans. Indigenous peoples had many thousands of years to develop distinctive cultures. From their perspective, they have lived in British Columbia "since time immemorial."

Europeans needed good reasons to make the arduous trip to British Columbia. It took up to half a year, travelling around the tip of South America, to reach its shores. The earliest outsiders arrived in the late 1700s out of curiosity or in search of a mythic Northwest Passage, which would make it possible to cross North America by water. Others came to trade for sea-otter or other animal furs. Only in the mid-1800s, two-thirds of a century later, did newcomers decide to stay.

**The Magnitude of British Columbia**

In a 1911 article entitled "British Columbia's Fifty-Seven Varieties," *British Columbia Magazine* astutely observed that "while there is only one British Columbia, there are so many kinds of it that he is a brave man indeed who can say he knows the province and get away with it."

British Columbia's vast emptiness, which forester-novelist Martin Allerdale Grainger termed "the great charm of life in uncivilized parts," has sometimes been its attraction. An early arrival in the Skeena Valley "delighted in a freedom that comes only in an untouched land." British Columbia promised escape from the world, for religious reasons as with Doukhobors and Mennonites, for the moral regeneration sought by Scandinavian idealists and many of the 1960s and '70s enthusiasts, or simply for the pleasure.

The remote location of BC has been both an advantage and a liability. The rest of Canada sometimes seems very far away. The province's longest-serving premier, W.A.C. Bennett, liked to say, "It's 3,000 miles from Vancouver to [the national capital of] Ottawa, but 30,000 from Ottawa to Vancouver." An earlier premier, John MacLean, offered the flip side of British Columbia's location in his far-sighted observation made in 1928 that "our sea frontage is the dominion's gateway to the Orient, with its swarming millions and untold possibilities for future trade."

**Once feared as killers, orca whales have become protected icons of wild nature.** *Photo Ian McAllister*

**Dawn breaks over a storm-washed beach along the Juan de Fuca Marine Trail on Vancouver Island.**

*Photo David Nunuk*

**In April 2006, the BC government created a 212-hectare (524-acre) conservancy to protect the habitat of the rare Kermode or spirit bear, recently declared BC's provincial mammal.** *Photo Ian McAllister*

Not just size and location but also BC's extravagant geography sets it apart. Painter and author Emily Carr repeatedly agonized over the character of her native province. It was only in middle age that she "stopped grieving about the isolation of the West. I believe now I was glad we were cut off." Carr struggled to make sense of British Columbia. "There is something bigger than fact: the underlying spirit, all it stands for, the mood, the vastness, the wildness, the Western breath of go-to-the-devil-if-you-don't-like-it, the eternal big spaceness of it. Oh the West! I'm of it and I love it." Returning home by train, she observed that "the air is denser and moister, the growth more dense and lush, the skies heavy and lowering (My hair is all curly on the edges with damp.)"

Other British Columbians have also found BC one of the world's favoured places in which to live. Writer Ethel Wilson reminisced in old age, "I have a life-long love for this province of ours which I share with many people, this British Columbia, as if it were a person, as it is, and a person of infinite variety and inference." For Tsleil-Waututh chief Leonard George, "if there is still an Eden in the world, it would be British Columbia."

Visitors have been equally enthusiastic. Approaching the Rocky Mountains heading toward the coast, English poet Rupert Brooke mused that "there is beauty here, at length, for the first time in Canada." Writer Stephen Leacock is said to have quipped, "British Columbia . . . If I had known what it was like, I wouldn't have been content with a mere visit. I'd have been born here."

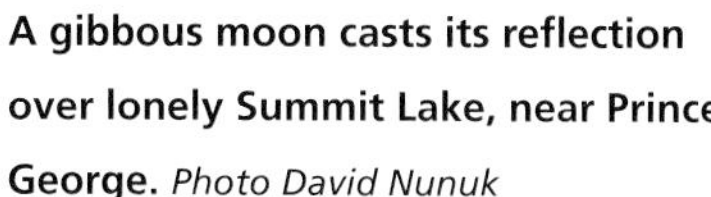

**A gibbous moon casts its reflection over lonely Summit Lake, near Prince George.** *Photo David Nunuk*

**Haida Gwaii's lush rainforest floor provides ideal habitat for mushrooms like the beautiful (but poisonous) *Amanita muscaria*.** *Photo David Nunuk*

A *Sunday Telegraph* headline of 2007 read, "Heaven on Earth British Columbia." The London newspaper gloried in how "[BC's] vast area incorporates a huge variety of majestic scenery."

The diverse landscapes, which appeal to residents and visitors alike, have not encouraged a strong sense of British Columbia as a single place. Many different peoples made up the indigenous or aboriginal population, and each spoke its own language. When Britain took charge of the future province in the mid-nineteenth century, it created not one but two separate colonies. Five years after their amalgamation in 1866, the united colony joined the young Canadian Confederation, but the change in status did not bring internal cohesion. The province's difficult terrain long continued to separate British Columbians from each other as well as from the rest of the country.

British Columbia extends 1,300 kilometres (800 miles) from north to south and some 800 kilometres (500 miles) from maritime coast to eastern mountains and prairie. The town of Atlin in the northwest is over 2,500 driving kilometres (1,550 miles) from Cranbrook in the southeast. Lying between the two communities are seemingly endless chains of mountains crossing the province from northwest to southeast. Their sharp peaks, steep slopes and narrow valleys have made isolation a major theme for many residents. These parallel ranges also create natural corridors running north and south, in direct opposition to BC's political status, based on links running east to the rest of Canada.

**Imagining the Coastline**
The long British Columbian coastline defies any single description. In *The Resurrection of Joseph Bourne,* which won the Governor General's Literary Award for Fiction in 1979, Jack Hodgins termed the coastline "the ragged green edge of the world." Long-time journalist Gwen Cash evoked "deep fjords twisting between precipitous cliffs, glaciers glistening on mountainous horizons, dark forests, tiny bays, enchanted islands, tumultuous tides."

Apart from mountains, BC's most prominent natural features are a long coastline and a vast interior plateau. Taking into account coastal islands—the largest are Vancouver Island and the Queen Charlotte Islands—BC has 25,000 kilometres (15,500 miles) of coastline. The water laps sandy beaches and washes up against sheer cliff faces. The coast's moderate but rainy climate encourages lush vegetation, including thick forests of coniferous (cone-bearing) cedar, fir, spruce and hemlock.

The interior plateau, which is bordered by the basins of the Fraser, Columbia, Skeena and Peace rivers, is the northern extension of the great North American Desert. This large plateau helps explain why, although over half of BC is forested, very little of the province is suitable for agriculture. Less than 3 percent is arable or potentially arable.

The coast and the interior could not be more different. Novelist Ethel Wilson described in *Swamp Angel* how "when you have reached Hope" in the eastern Fraser Valley, "you are entering a continent, and you meet the continent there, at Hope."

British Columbia's large size and diverse terrain mean the province is often divided into regions; during much of the twentieth century, the federal census divided it into ten regions. These useful divisions continue in modified forms for administrative purposes ranging from weather forecasting to tourist promotion.

**This ancient Sitka spruce in Carmanah–Walbran Provincial Park was already large enough to dwarf human admirers when the colony of British Columbia was created in 1858.**
*Photo Chris Cheadle*

YUKON
TERRITORY
NORTHWEST
TERRITORIES
ALASKA
ALASKA BORDER
PACIFIC
OCEAN
ALBERTA
WASHINGTON
IDAHO
MONTANA
N
Atlin
Dease Lake
Stikine R
Liard R
Muncho Lake
Fort Nelson
Stewart
Portland Canal
Nass R
Skeena R
Williston L
Hudson's Hope
Peace R
Fort St. John
Dawson Creek
Tumbler Ridge
Masset
Prince Rupert
Smithers
Terrace
Babine L
Stuart L
Skidegate
Kitimat
Hazelton
Fort St. James
Hecate Strait
HAIDA GWAII
(QUEEN CHARLOTTE
ISLANDS)
Ootsa L
Vanderhoof
Prince George
Fraser R
Quesnel
Barkerville
Mt. Robson
Bella Coola
Bella Bella
Bella Coola R
Queen
Charlotte
Sound
Quesnel L
Kinbasket L
Williams Lake
Mt. Waddington
100 Mile House
Clearwater
Columbia R
Port Hardy
Golden
Lillooet
Thompson R
Salmon
Arm
Revelstoke
Campbell River
Powell
River
Kamloops
VANCOUVER
ISLAND
Whistler
Comox
Merritt
Vernon
Harrison L
Kelowna
Arrow Lakes
Kootenay L
Tofino
Strait of Georgia
Vancouver
Okanagan L
Nanaimo
Hope
Nelson
Kimberley
Abbotsford
Penticton
Cranbrook
Fernie
Juan de Fuca Strait
Victoria
Trail
THE REGIONS OF
BRITISH COLUMBIA
Prince Rupert & the Northwest
Peace River & the Northeast
Prince George & the Central Interior
Bella Coola & the Central Coast
Kamloops & the Southern Interior
Victoria, Vancouver Island & the Gulf Islands
Vancouver & the Fraser Valley
Kelowna & the Okanagan/Boundary
West Kootenay
East Kootenay

# PRINCE GEORGE AND THE CENTRAL INTERIOR

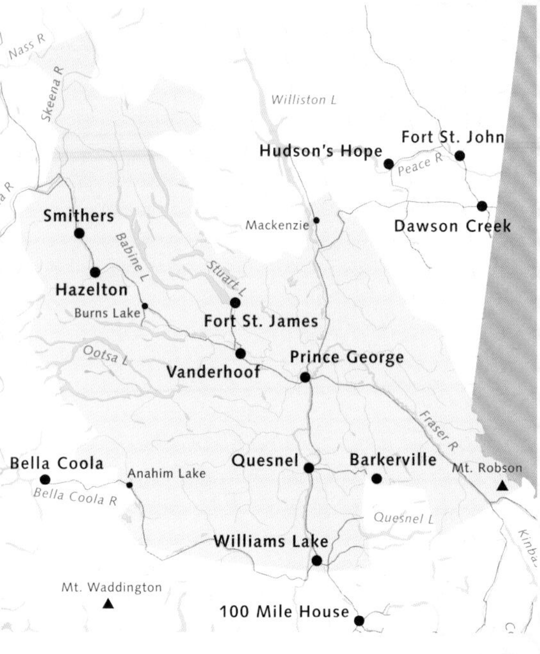


The Central Interior, the geographical heart of the province, is part of BC's vast interior plateau. It is also in many ways the birthplace of modern British Columbia, since it was into this richly endowed area of lakes and rivers occupied by the Dakelh (Carrier) people that the first non-aboriginals came to live year-round for years on end at the trading posts of Fort Fraser, Fort St. James and Fort George—later Prince George—all founded in the early 1800s by the fur trader Simon Fraser. A century later a rail link west from the prairies to newly established Prince Rupert opened up the Central Interior to agriculture, although it was forestry that built the region's strong economy. Prince George, styled the Spruce Capital of Canada, came into its own with the growth of the forest industry after World War II and by the 1980s had grown from a rough mill town to the major manufacturing, supply, government and educational centre for north-central British Columbia. Fort St. James, Vanderhoof, Burns Lake, Houston and Smithers are other important communities in the area. The region's southern third contains the forestry centre of Quesnel and the gold-rush boom town of Barkerville, and forms the northern part of the Cariboo.

**Above: Situated at the confluence of the Nechako and Fraser rivers, Prince George lies in the traditional territory of the Lheit-Lit'en people, a subgroup of the Dakelh. With a population of seventy thousand, it is the undisputed hub of central BC.** *Photo Lenard Sanders*

**Left: The Two Rivers Gallery has added a new dimension to Prince George cultural life.** *Photo Keith Douglas*

**Connaught Hill Park offers an impressive panoramic view of Prince George.**
*Photo Lenard Sanders*

Right: **The old truss rail bridge across the Fraser River has been a Prince George landmark since it was built by the Grand Trunk Pacific Railway in 1914.** *Photo Lenard Sanders*

Bottom right: **The impressive hilltop campus of the University of Northern British Columbia, opened in 1994, has given Prince George an architectural centrepiece.** *Photo Keith Douglas*

Below: **The Exploration Place Science Centre and Museum, opened in 2001, is the focus of many Prince George cultural activities.** *Photo J.F. Bergeron*

**Williams Lake**

Williams Lake, located in Shuswap (Secwepemc) territory, is known as the hub of the Cariboo and is the largest centre between Kamloops and Prince George. Long associated with ranching, it was for many years the largest cattle-shipping point in BC and hosts a famous stampede, although forestry is now the leading industry.

**Viewing the Fur Trade**

Indigenous peoples and visitors from the outside world began their ongoing contact in British Columbia during the fur trade. A handful of men lived in small posts, intent on enticing their neighbours to trade animal pelts for the European goods they had to offer. Local peoples were equally determined to use the trade to their advantage. The dynamics of this exchange come to life at the restored Fort St. James in the Central Interior and Fort Langley in the Fraser Valley. Visitors are introduced to a very different BC than today's familiar province.

Above: **A Dakelh woman stands outside the Hudson's Bay Company General Warehouse & Fur Store at the Fort St. James National Historic Site, built in 1888.** *Photo Rick Blacklaws*

Top: **The village of Hazelton is situated on the banks of the mighty Skeena River.** *Photo Chris Jaksa*

Left: **Fort St. James, a thriving central BC village today, was founded in the early days of the fur trade.** *Photo Chris Jaksa*

Above: **The viewpoint at Pinnacles Park is an hour's hike from Quesnel.**
*Photo Chris Harris*

Top: **Central BC is moose country.**
*Photo Chris Harris*

Right: **Central BC is world renowned for its wonderful lake trout fishing.**
*Photo Keith Douglas*

**The rich bottomland of the Bulkley Valley attracted farmers and ranchers from early times.** *Photo Keith Douglas*

**Reliving the Gold Rush**

The gold rush lives on at Barkerville. The Cariboo boom town of the 1860s is the largest historic site in British Columbia. Visitors can tread wooden sidewalks once chockablock with miners glorying in their new-found wealth, be entertained by hurdy-gurdy dancers intent on parting the miners from their fortunes, and pan for gold much as miners did 150 years ago.

**The main street of Barkerville, once the heart of the Cariboo gold rush, serves as a fascinating monument to the phenomenon that led to the formation of British Columbia in 1858.** *Photo Chris Harris*

**Sunrise on Babcock Lake in Bowron Lake Provincial Park, near Barkerville.** *Photo Chris Harris*

# Peace River and the Northeast

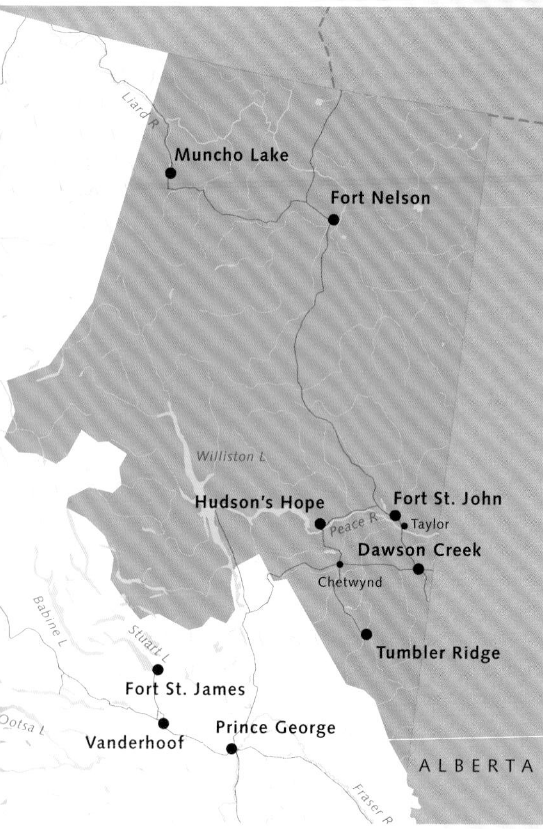


The next of British Columbia's ten regions is the Northeast, lying on the far side of the Rockies, which otherwise form the province's eastern boundary. Since this mountain range symbolizes BC's separation from the rest of Canada, it leaves the Northeast an orphan. The region is, to quote anthropologist Hugh Brody, "not even a name but a geographer's indefinite description. Its three worlds—foothills, muskeg and prairie—long remained beyond outsiders' grasp."

The agricultural potential of the Northeast's southern third, named for the Peace River flowing east into Alberta, was realized during the interwar years once it became accessible by rail from the prairies. Extremely hot in summer and cold in winter, the Peace presented both an opportunity and a challenge. The area north of the Peace, climatically too harsh for farming, drew few outsiders until Americans constructed the Alaska Highway across the region during World War II. An oil and natural-gas boom after the war has extended settlement.

Below: **The annual Dawson Creek Stampede, complete with thrilling chuckwagon races, celebrates the ranching heritage of the Peace River country.** *Photo Don Pettit*

**Above: The historic grain elevator that serves as the information centre and museum for Dawson Creek and area.** *Photo Don Pettit*

Harvesting oats near Dawson Creek. The Peace River country is justly known as BC's breadbasket.

*Photo David Nunuk*

DAWSON CREEK
FT. ST. JOHN 49
FT. NELSON 300
WHITEHORSE 918
FAIRBANKS 1523
MILE "0"
ALASKA
HIGHWAY

### Settlements of the Northeast

When the first European fur traders ventured into the Northeast region, they set up a string of posts, some of them fairly ephemeral. Several short-lived posts existed from 1794 onwards near Fort St. John, now the largest community north of Prince George and the centre of the Peace River area. In 1805 Simon Fraser founded Rocky Mountain Portage House near present-day Hudson's Hope, home to the huge W.A.C. Bennett Dam on the Peace River. Fort Nelson, also established by Fraser, is a booming forestry and oil and gas centre. Dawson Creek was not a fur-trade fort, but began as a market town in 1907. Today it is famous as Mile 0 of the Alaska Highway and for grain farming.

Far left: **The northern lights are a source of continual wonder in northern BC.**
*Photo John E. Marriott*

Left: **Dawson Creek is proud of its position as Mile 0 of the 2,414-kilometre (1,500-mile) Alaska Highway.**
*Photo Don Pettit*

Below: **The sun sets over Sheerdale Landing on the Peace River.**
*Photo Don Pettit*

Above: **Bighorn sheep are abundant in BC's Rocky Mountains.** *Photo Jared Hobbs*

Top right: **In the Peace River country, winter is something to be savoured. Here children explore an ice sculpture at the High on Ice Winter Carnival in Fort St. John.** *Photo courtesy of City of Fort St. John*

**Liard River Hot Springs Provincial Park in northern BC is a much-visited natural wonder.** *Photo David Nunuk*

**The Alaska Highway, built for strategic purposes during World War II, now serves as the overland lifeline to the Yukon and Alaska and is well travelled by tourists.** *Photo John E. Marriott*

# PRINCE RUPERT AND THE NORTHWEST

The Northwest region extends from the southern tip of the Queen Charlotte Islands to the province's northern boundary at 60°N, excluding the long coastal strip formed by the Alaska Panhandle. The region has the longest history of human habitation, as many historians believe British Columbia's First Peoples came this way after crossing the Bering Strait. Most later arrivals have simply passed through, as with the 1898 Klondike gold rush to the Yukon. A harsh climate and difficult terrain have discouraged their staying. Permanent settlements are restricted to indigenous peoples, a handful of resource-based towns such as Terrace and Kitimat, and the coastal port of Prince Rupert.

Set in the heart of territory where the powerful Tsimshian once ruled supreme, Prince Rupert was designed as the Pacific terminus of the Grand Trunk Pacific Railway and

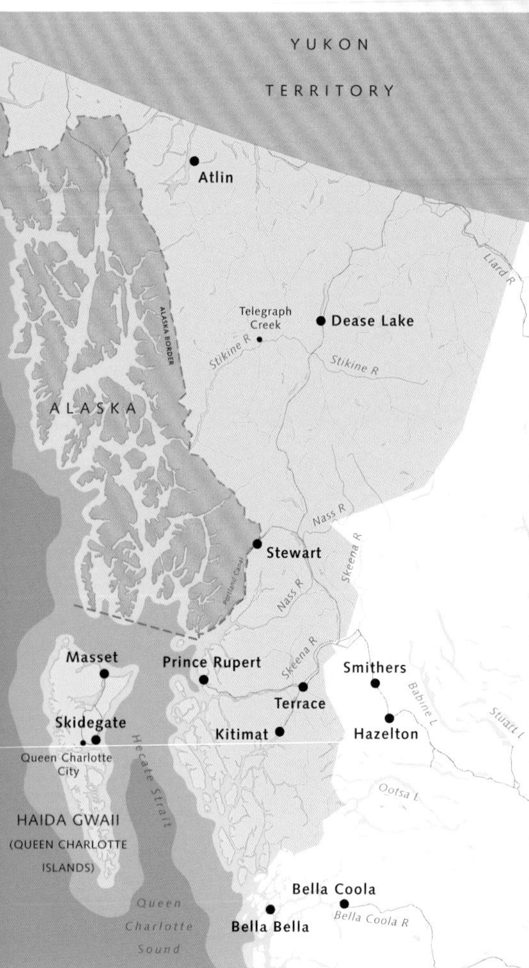

**Top right: The Haida Heritage Centre at Quay'llnagaay near Skidegate, Haida Gwaii, is a place for nurturing Haida culture and sharing it with the rest of the world.** *Photo Lonnie Wishart*

## Haida Gwaii

The Haida who live on the Queen Charlotte Islands know it as Haida Gwaii, which means "islands of the people" in their language. Once said to number fourteen thousand in a hundred villages, the Haida were reduced to fewer than six hundred by the early 1900s, because of epidemics and other effects of European contact. Today there are almost four thousand Haida; just under fifteen hundred live on their two reserves located at Skidegate and Old Massett. In 1993 the Haida signed an agreement with the federal government to co-manage the new Gwaii Haanas National Park covering the southern third of Haida Gwaii.

Top left: **Kunghit Haida totems in Ninstints (Skungwa'ai) village, Haida Gwaii.** *Photo David Nunuk*

Left: **Forest scene, Haida Gwaii. Lush growth typifies the Queen Charlotte archipelago.** *Photo David Nunuk*

expected by its founders to become a great seaport rivalling Vancouver. Instead it developed into a commercial fishing centre, surrounded by canneries serving the great salmon runs on the nearby Skeena and Nass rivers. In recent years the fisheries have gone into precipitous decline, as have the many lumber mills that also once drove the Rupert economy. However, the vision of the founders may yet prove the seaport city's salvation. Prince Rupert is some thirty hours closer to the booming markets of Asia than ports to the south and the city's deep, world-class port facilities are expanding rapidly to keep up with demand.

Right: **Prince Rupert celebrates its maritime heritage each June with the annual Seafest festival.** *Photo Shaun Thomas*

Below: **The Prince Rupert waterfront at Cow Bay.** *Photo Lonnie Wishart*

Left: **Prince Rupert's expanding container terminal and its position on the shortest sea–land route between Asia and the American Midwest bode well for its future as a major seaport.** *Photo courtesy of the Prince Rupert Port Authority*

Below: **Dusk illumines Prince Rupert's busy deep-sea grain terminal.** *Photo Chris Cheadle*

**A March snowstorm blankets a commercial fish-boat marina in Haida Gwaii.**

*Photo David Nunuk*

LUXANA
SKIL JADA

Above: **River rafting at Kluane/ Wrangell–St. Elias/Glacier Bay/Tatshenshini–Alsek UNESCO World Heritage Site.** *Photo Bruce Obee*

Right: **A Nisga'a boy dons dancing regalia, Nass River Valley.** *Photo Chris Cheadle*

Left: **Atlin, a small village in BC's extreme northwest, is famous for its spectacular lakes.** *Photo J.A. Kraulis*

Below: **The Tatshenshini-Alsek Park contains nearly one million hectares (2.5 million acres) of magnificent natural landscapes in the very northwest corner of British Columbia.** *Photo John E. Marriott*

# BELLA COOLA AND THE CENTRAL COAST

The Central Coast lies south of the Northwest region. European penetration of the Central Coast has been restricted to cannery and logging communities, such long-time company towns as Powell River and Ocean Falls, and idealistic enclaves like Sointula, Cape Scott and Bella Coola, founded by dreamers who wanted to make a fresh start in a new country. In her travel classic *The Curve of Time,* Muriel Blanchet recounted summers from 1927 to 1942 spent exploring coastal coves and inlets with her children in their small cedar cruiser *Caprice.* Blanchet quickly observed that, in spite of its pockets of settlers, the Central Coast was still largely uninhabited except for indigenous peoples.

Below: **A pair of eagles perch in a tree above the Bella Coola River.** *Photo Michael Wigle*

**Above: Mountain-walled Bella Coola Valley, ancestral home of the Nuxalk Nation, was the western terminus of Alexander Mackenzie's historic overland crossing of North America in 1793. Now a small farming and forestry community, Bella Coola has an irresistible charm.** *Photo Michael Wigle*

**Top right: A pastoral scene near the western boundary of Tweedsmuir Provincial Park in the Bella Coola Valley.** *Photo Michael Wigle*

A heli-skier soars above South Bentinck Arm near Bella Coola.
*Photo Jan Condon*

**Worlds unto Themselves**
For over 50 years the largest settlement in the Bella Coola-Central Coast area was Ocean Falls, a company town attached to a pulp mill in nearby Cousins Inlet. Company towns like Ocean Falls and Powell River, at the south end of the region, were worlds unto themselves. The company that owned the town exercised virtually unlimited authority over the lives of workers and their families, but made up for this by offering modern housing with electricity and indoor plumbing, sports and leisure facilities, good health care and good schools. Today Powell River contains British Columbia's only National Historic District, a heritage showcase comprising thirty commercial structures and four hundred homes constructed for workers between 1910 and 1930, with the still-operating mill as an authentic backdrop.

Above: **A logger manhandles rigging in the Bella Coola Valley.**
*Photo Patrick Armstrong*

Top right: **There is nothing like salmon prepared the traditional Nuxalk way.**
*Photo Keith Pootlass*

Right: **In spawning season Pacific salmon return to Central Coast rivers in great numbers, making them an ideal food source for First Nations.**
*Photo Ian McAllister*

Left: **Coastal grizzly bears depend on the fall salmon runs for survival.** *Photo Michael Wigle*

Below: **Mountain-shrouded valleys like Bella Coola make for very short days in winter.** *Photo Michael Wigle*

Above: **A hiker pauses along the Turner Lake Trail in Tweedsmuir Park to enjoy a breathtaking view of Hunlen Falls, one of the highest in Canada.** *Photo Chris Harris*

Left: **The Rainbow Range in Tweedsmuir Park is a stunning geological phenomenon.** *Photo Vance Hanna*

Right: **The nicely restored Provincial Building is a part of the old Powell River townsite, a designated National Historic District.** *Photo Keith A. Thirkell*

Below: **Saltwater estuaries like this one at the head of Knight Inlet play a key role in the web of coastal life.** *Photo Chris Cheadle*

Opposite: **The spire of Mount Denman looms above a kayaker paddling the calm waters of Desolation Sound, a boater's mecca.** *Photo Chris Jaksa*

# Kamloops and the Southern Interior

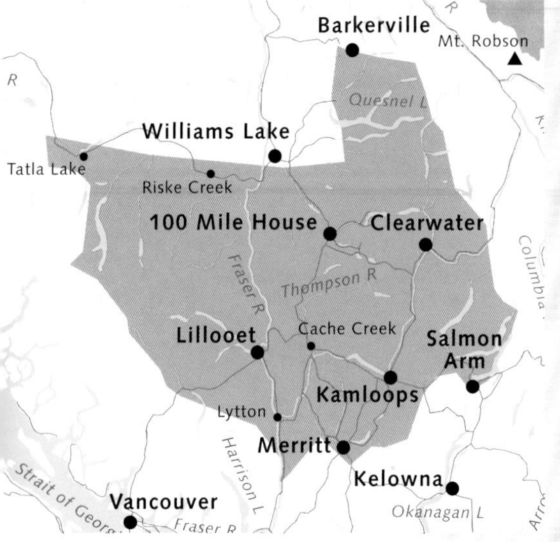


South of the Central Interior runs a major transportation corridor known as the Southern Interior. Indigenous peoples long used the region's rivers to trade. The Southern Interior's principal city of Kamloops originated as a fur-trade post. Routes to the mid-nineteenth-century gold strikes, as they moved north into the Cariboo, crossed this region. North of the boom town of Lillooet, the names of roadhouses incorporated the distances in early communities such as 70 Mile House and 100 Mile House.

Large stretches of open range and grassland make much of the Southern Interior suitable for raising cattle. The Cariboo of gold-rush fame is now given over to ranching. The area west of the Fraser River is called the Chilcotin.

Left: **The lower reaches of the Thompson River near Lytton are among the province's favoured whitewater kayaking and rafting areas.**
*Photo Chris Cheadle*

Opposite: **Strategically located at the confluence of the North and South Thompson rivers, Kamloops has been a Southern Interior transportation hub since the days of the fur trade.**
*Photo Kelly Funk*

Cowboying is still a viable profession in the Southern Interior.
*Photo David Nunuk*

**Cowboy Country**

The Southern Interior early on became cowboy country. Some pioneer ranchers were unsuccessful gold rushers, like the one Alex Bulman describes in his book, *Kamloops Cattlemen*: "He, like many others, did not find gold in the gravel and had gone into the freighting business on the Cariboo road from Yale. He had saved his money, and bought himself a few cattle which soon grew into a herd. Running them on freerange was fine at the start, but he had bought land at Cherry Creek and, by 1886, had built up a pretty good outfit." While many ranchers were satisfied with two to three hundred head of cattle, some aspired to more. The Douglas Lake Cattle Company in the Nicola Valley was organized as a syndicate in 1882 to supply railway construction gangs with beef. By 1886 it comprised 900 hectares (2,250 acres) running 12,000 head of cattle. Owned for a time by the Woodward family of department store fame, Douglas Lake Ranch operates today under American ownership. The general store in one of the original ranch buildings is open to passersby.

Above: **A rock climber scales an outcrop above Kamloops Lake. British Columbia offers endless opportunities for outdoor adventure.** *Photo Kelly Funk*

Right: **Each spring the male sharp-tailed grouse returns to the grasslands near Kamloops to perform a mating dance for the females.** *Photo Jared Hobbs*

Left: **Majestic Helmcken Falls in Wells Gray Provincial Park plunges 141 metres (462 feet), almost three times higher than Niagara Falls.** *Photo John E. Marriott*

Below: **Pioneer ranchers could hardly believe their eyes when they first saw the open grasslands of the Cariboo-Chilcotin.** *Photo Vance Hanna*

# West and East Kootenays

East of the Southern Interior are the mountainous West Kootenay and East Kootenay regions. Rugged heights are intersected by major rivers that widen into lakes. The West Kootenay region centres on Arrow and Kootenay lakes; the East Kootenay region, which abuts on the neighbouring province of Alberta, centres on the Columbia River.

As with the Northeast region, the Kootenays' geography has isolated them from the rest of British Columbia. The language spoken by the Ktunaxa people prior to contact with outsiders has no linguistic relatives, which suggests that the culture developed independently. American entrepreneurs coming north during the 1890s set off a mining boom that opened the two regions to settlement. Today the Kootenays are prized for recreation and retirement.

Left: **Nelson, once known as the Queen of the Kootenays, is one of BC's most charming cities.**
*Photo Steve Ogle*

Opposite top: **Two mountain bikers on Idaho Peak with Valhalla Range behind, Slocan Valley, Kootenays. Outdoor recreation is one of the Kootenays' leading attractions.**
*Photo Steve Ogle*

Opposite bottom: **In autumn, the golden foliage of the larch provides Kootenay forests with one of their trademark images. View from Opabin Plateau with Mount Huber in the background.**
*Photo John E. Marriott*

## The Resourceful Ktunaxa People

The Kootenays' geography helps to explain why the Ktunaxa language is unique and its culture so distinctive. Under the leadership of Chief Sophie Pierre, the Ktunaxa have taken back St. Eugene Mission, a residential school that taught more than five thousand children between 1910 and 1970. Once a symbol of oppression that threatened to take their culture away, it is now restored as a major tourist site, inviting visitors from around the world to learn about the Ktunaxa culture.

Top right: **The St. Eugene Mission Resort near Cranbrook is a spectacular hotel, casino and golf facility built around a former mission school by the Ktunaxa and two other First Nations.** *Photo Don Weixl*

Right: **Hub of the Elk Valley coal-mining district, Fernie burned in 1908 but was rebuilt in durable stone and brick buildings that give Second Avenue its turn-of-the-century charm. Fernie Alpine Resort and Lizard Range rise in the background.** *Photo Henry Georgi*

Above: **The city hall at Kaslo, built in 1898, is one of many well-preserved heritage structures that draw crowds of admirers to the lakeside village.** *Photo Bruce Obee*

Left: **A ridge in the heart of the Bugaboo Spires, East Kootenay.** *Photo David Nunuk*

Below: **Sinclair Canyon, Kootenay National Park, makes for a dramatic entry into the small mountain town of Radium Hot Springs.** *Photo Barrett & Mackay*

**Mount Assiniboine and Sunburst Peak with Sunburst and Cerulean lakes, an icon of the BC Rockies.**

*Photo David Nunuk*

# KELOWNA AND THE OKANAGAN/BOUNDARY

West of the Kootenays is the Okanagan/Boundary region, which also extends south to the American border. Its central feature is Okanagan Lake, which runs 130 kilometres (76 miles) north and south with subsidiary lakes at either end. An early visitor waxed enthusiastic over the region's possibilities, reporting a "profusion of grass that covers both woodland and meadow, affording rich pastures for domestic animals." At the beginning of the twentieth century the Okanagan Valley caught the attention of British immigrants and others who grew fruit in irrigated orchards. More recently the region has become a centre of wine production. The market town of Kelowna is today a major metropolis.

**The SS *Sicamous*, a historic CPR sternwheeler that once plied Okanagan waterways, now the centrepiece of the Okanagan Inland Marine Heritage Park at Penticton. A city of beautiful beaches between two of BC's most popular recreational lakes, Penticton is a favourite with vacationers.** *Photo Russ Heinl*

**Kelowna is the largest city in the Okanagan/Boundary region and the largest urban centre outside the Lower Mainland.** *Photo courtesy Tourism Kelowna-SATW*

Left: **The Gatzke Farm near Kelowna. Apple trees were first planted in the Okanagan Valley in 1859, presaging its destiny as a major fruit-growing area. Recently, vineyards have begun to displace the trademark orchards.**
*Photo courtesy Tourism Kelowna*

Below: **Predator Ridge Golf Resort Community is just one of the many attractions that make Vernon, like the Okanagan/Boundary in general, one of the province's most popular recreation and retirement destinations.** *Photo David Nunuk*

**Okanagan Vineyards**
The wine produced in Okanagan vineyards has increasingly been recognized around the world. The most sought-after item is the pricey ice wine. "Serve some chilled ice wine from, say, Canada's Okanagan Valley, and I promise you'll evolve instantly from croaker to crown prince," the *New York Times* gushed in 2006.

This picture-perfect estate winery near Oliver is one of more than sixty Okanagan wineries known to connoisseurs of fine wine around the world.
*Photo David Nunuk*

Above: **Parasailing over Osoyoos Lake.**

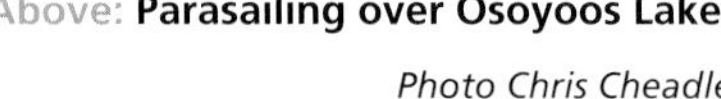

*Photo Chris Cheadle*

Top right: **Sculpture at Nk´Mip Desert Cultural Centre, an interpretive centre featuring Canada's only true desert, operated by the Osoyoos Indian Band.**
*Photo Chris Cheadle*

Right: **A fruit stand in Keremeos displays a bountiful autumn harvest of pumpkins and squash.** *Photo David Nunuk*

**Spotted Lake, a unique drying alkali lake in the South Okanagan.** *Photo David Nunuk*

# VANCOUVER AND THE FRASER VALLEY

In British Columbia's southwest corner is the Lower Mainland region, which extends south to the international boundary and north up Howe Sound through the Sechelt Peninsula. To the east it runs along the valley of the Fraser River past the one-time fur-trade post of Fort Langley as far as the community of Hope. Especially attractive to small farmers, the fertile Fraser Valley is the most intensely cultivated area of British Columbia.

The discovery of gold in sandbars in the Fraser River in 1858 drew large numbers of non-aboriginal people to British Columbia for the first time. The gold rush moved the British government to bestow colonial status on the mainland, giving it the name British Columbia. Its capital was initially Fort Langley, but was soon moved to New Westminster.

Vancouver came into being when the transcontinental Canadian Pacific Railway was completed in 1886 and its western terminus was sited on the great natural harbour formed by Burrard Inlet, just north of the Fraser delta. The new city's name honoured the British explorer who had visited there almost a century earlier.

Rapidly growing Vancouver soon dominated the Lower Mainland and then the province as a whole. The city's linkages extended into the prairies and west to Asia. From the 1920s onward the Lower Mainland region contained over half the province's population.

Richmond, located immediately south of Vancouver, has changed the most dramatically of any municipality in British Columbia over the past three decades. Its population has doubled to 175,000, almost wholly through immigration. Until the early 1980s Richmond consisted of farms and wetlands with a smattering of housing developments. By 2006 Richmond had the highest proportion of visible minorities—65 percent, over two-thirds of them Chinese—of any city in Canada. Fewer than 1 percent of schoolchildren spoke English as a second language three decades earlier, but by 2001 half did so.

**British Columbia's Largest City**

Vancouver is British Columbia's largest and most prominent city. Its metropolitan area, known as Metro Vancouver, comprises several large municipalities including West Vancouver, North Vancouver, Burnaby, Coquitlam, New Westminster, Surrey, Langley, Richmond and Delta, with a combined population of over two million people.

Left and below left: **Comparison of downtown Vancouver as seen from the Granville Street Bridge. The top image was photographed in 1958 and the bottom image was captured forty-six years later in 2004.**

*Photos Fred Herzog, courtesy of Equinox Gallery*

Opposite: **Historic Hells Gate squeezes the mighty Fraser River into a narrow thirty-metre (one-hundred-foot) gorge, a dangerous obstacle to rafters and migrating salmon but a thrilling sight from the overhead air tram.**

*Photo Rick Blacklaws*

**Greater Vancouver and the North Shore Mountains resplendent under an early morning dusting of snow.** *Photo Jeff Birch*

Right and far right: **A Sikh woman and man attend the Vaisakhi Nagar Keertan (neighbourhood celebration) in Surrey.** *Photos Pardeep Singh*

Below: **A dairy farm near Deroche in the Fraser Valley, British Columbia's richest mixed farming area.**
*Photo Mike Grandmaison*

Cultural amenities have grown apace. The first of a clutch of upscale shopping centres catering to Asian tastes opened in Richmond in 1990. Their varied styles reflect the taste differences among immigrants from Hong Kong to Taiwan to mainland China. Once "plain Jane" without Vancouver's big-city gloss, Richmond has become a Eurasian metropolis reminiscent of Honolulu or Hong Kong.

British Columbia's second-largest city is one of the province's best-kept secrets, being overshadowed by proximity to Vancouver. Surrey's dispersed character means there is no city centre that compares to its more prominent neighbour's. Over 300 square kilometres (about 116 square miles) in size, Surrey is suburban rather than urban. Almost 400,000 people live there, mostly in nicely maintained homes in easy reach of neighbourhood shopping centres serving their everyday needs.

**Vancouver's New Dynamic**

Vancouver's new dynamic did not just happen. Two factors came together. The first is extensive middle-class immigration from Asia. By 2006, almost half of Vancouverites claimed Asian descent. Alongside a more sophisticated range of newspapers, television channels, supermarkets and restaurants are such beloved festivals as the annual Dragon Boat Races and Chinese New Year parade. The second is Vancouver City Council's determination to create a more livable city. A mix of business and residential development has so transformed the False Creek, Yaletown and Coal Harbour areas that Vancouver is repeatedly acclaimed as the most livable city in the world.

Above: **A drummer entertains at the Taiwanese Cultural Festival in Vancouver's Chinatown.** *Photo Reza Sheydaei*

Left: **Sunset over the riverside community of Steveston in Richmond, for many years a Japanese Canadian centre and home port to British Columbia's largest commercial salmon-fishing fleet.** *Photo David Nunuk*

**Black Tusk in Garibaldi Provincial Park near Whistler, a volcanic pinnacle towering 2,319 metres (7,600 feet) above sea level, is the province's most frequently climbed peak.** *Photo David Nunuk*

# Victoria, Vancouver Island and The Gulf Islands

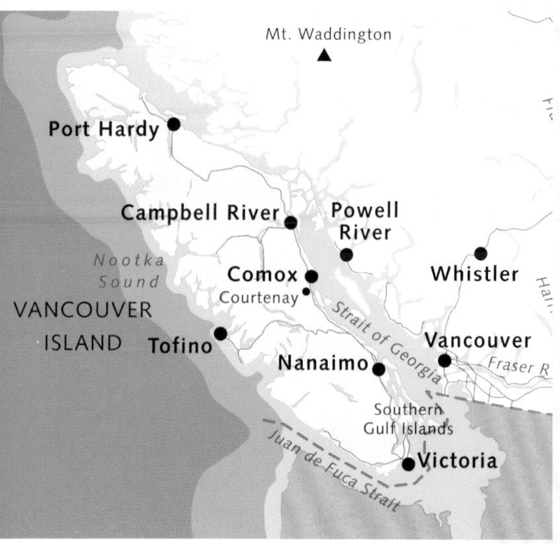


The last of the ten regions of British Columbia consists of Vancouver Island and the adjacent Gulf Islands. Descending from a mountainous backbone running north and south, Vancouver Island has a rugged west coast but an east coast with some fertile lowland suitable for agriculture. Many of the earliest encounters between British Columbia's First Peoples and newcomers occurred in the late 1700s on Vancouver Island's west coast at Nootka Sound.

The fur-trading Hudson's Bay Company arrived on Vancouver Island in 1843, and within the decade employees had settled down at Fort Victoria on the Island's southern tip. In 1849 Vancouver Island was made a British colony, with Victoria its capital. A large natural harbour at nearby Esquimalt served for nearly half a century as the home base for Britain's Royal Navy operations on the west coast of North and South America. Just over a hundred kilometres (sixty miles) northeast of Victoria lies Nanaimo, the Island's second-largest city, which first came to the interest of Europeans because of its rich coal deposits. On British Columbia's entry into Confederation with Canada in 1871, Victoria became the provincial capital.

Some 225 Gulf Islands dot the Strait of Georgia lying between Vancouver Island and the mainland of British Columbia. The most populous of these is Salt Spring Island, which attracted newcomers almost as early as Vancouver Island. The smallest of the islands are uninhabited specks. While the larger islands such as Salt Spring, Gabriola and Denman contain patches of farmland, the Gulf Islands are mostly rocky.

A pleasant climate, attractive settings and cultural amenities have made Vancouver Island and the Gulf Islands a recreation and retirement destination for Canadians from across the country. The four Canadian municipalities with populations over five thousand and the highest median ages in 2006—between fifty-five and sixty-one years—are all located there.

**The Face of Victoria**

By the early twentieth century the provincial capital of Victoria had acquired the profile it still possesses a century later. The Legislative Buildings were erected during the 1890s and the nearby Empress Hotel in the next decade. By then Victoria had taken a secondary position to Vancouver and was assuming the more genteel bearing it presents to the world today.

Above: **A Nuu-chah-nulth man from Vancouver Island's west coast in traditional dress.** *Photo Chris Cheadle*

Left: **Ganges, Salt Spring Island's largest community, offers summer visitors a tempting array of shopping and dining pleasures.** *Photo Boomer Jerritt*

Opposite: **Victoria's famous Inner Harbour, with the Fairmont Empress Hotel on the left, the Legislative Buildings on the right and flowers everywhere.** *Photo Roy Ooms*

Right: **The east coast of Vancouver Island is home to some well-established dairy farms.** *Photo Dave Blackey*

Below: **The fantastically sculpted Malaspina Galleries on Gabriola Island, named for the Spanish explorer Alejandro Malaspina, are typical of scenic sandstone formations found throughout the southern Gulf Islands.** *Photo Chris Cheadle*

Far left: **The soft corals and sponges make a brilliant display in Browning Pass, a world-class scuba-diving destination near Port Hardy.** *Photo Dale Sanders*

Left: **A carved sign welcomes Port Hardy visitors from both sea and shore.** *Photo Chris Cheadle*

Below: **A breathtaking view of Mt. Albert Edward and Strathcona Park as seen from the chairlift at Mount Washington.** *Photo Chris Cheadle*

**The broad, ocean-washed sands of Long Beach in Pacific Rim National Park on the west coast of Vancouver Island are among the province's prime recreational attractions.** *Photo Chris Cheadle*

### The Wild Edge

On the west coast of Vancouver Island, the Pacific Ocean truly makes its presence known. The rain-laden storms that batter remote indigenous villages, the much-walked West Coast Trail, Pacific Rim National Park and the favoured tourist destination of Tofino all provide a powerful reminder that in British Columbia nature is still in charge. Precisely for this reason, the temperate rainforests containing some of Canada's largest trees flourish there and elsewhere along the coast. The sun returns, and for a moment it seems as if the views along endless beaches do in fact reach to Asia.

**Kayakers in the Broken Group Islands off the west coast of Vancouver Island share the scenery with a herd of sea lions.** *Photo Chris Cheadle*

**Remote, windswept Triangle Island off the north coast of Vancouver Island is an important bird sanctuary.**
*Photo Russ Heinl*

**Picturesque Telegraph Cove on northern Vancouver Island was once a sawmill settlement but now serves as a whale-watching base. It is typical of shorefront villages that once dotted the British Columbia coast.**

*Photo Chris Cheadle*

TELEGRAPH COVE

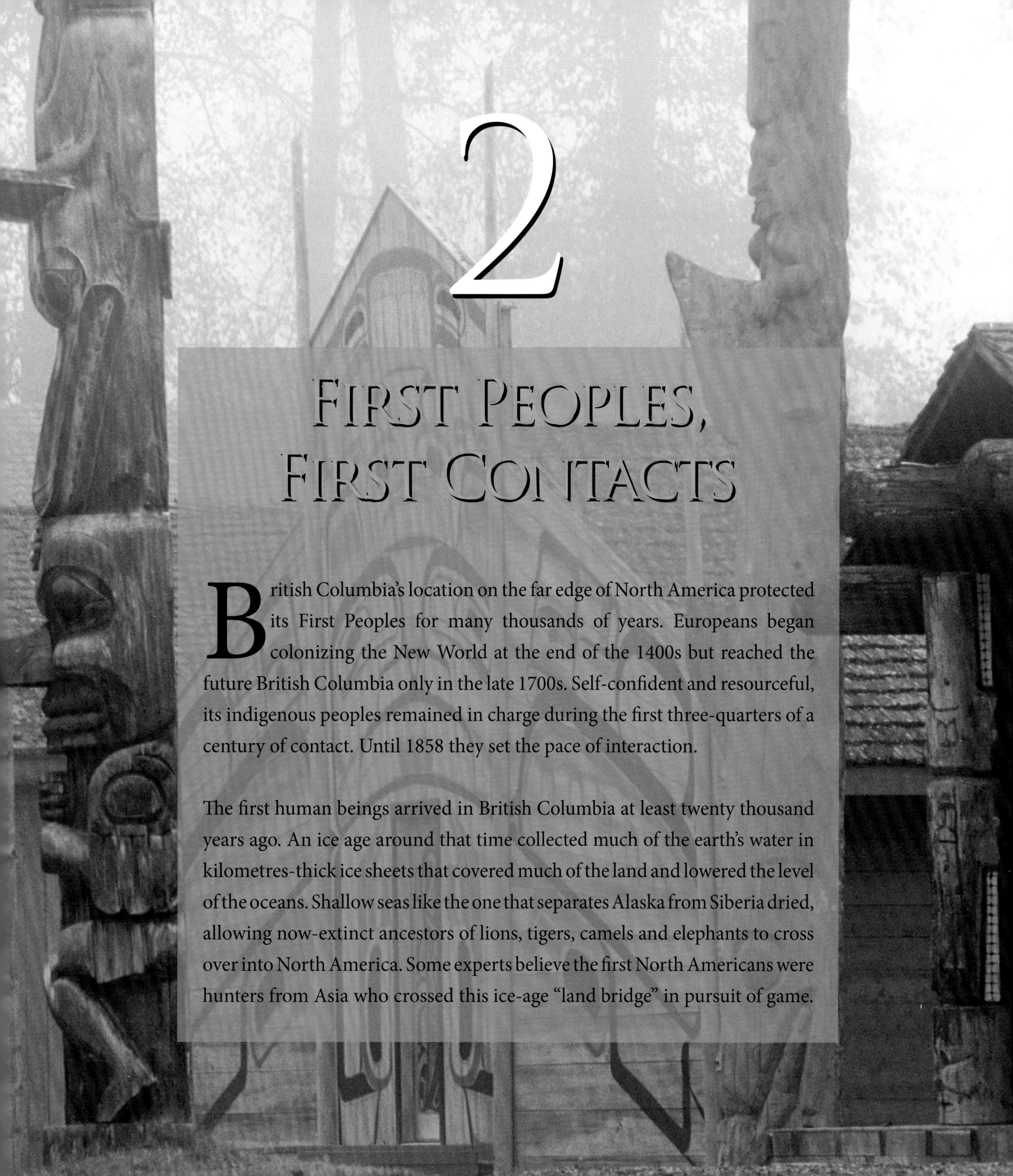

# 2

# First Peoples, First Contacts

British Columbia's location on the far edge of North America protected its First Peoples for many thousands of years. Europeans began colonizing the New World at the end of the 1400s but reached the future British Columbia only in the late 1700s. Self-confident and resourceful, its indigenous peoples remained in charge during the first three-quarters of a century of contact. Until 1858 they set the pace of interaction.

The first human beings arrived in British Columbia at least twenty thousand years ago. An ice age around that time collected much of the earth's water in kilometres-thick ice sheets that covered much of the land and lowered the level of the oceans. Shallow seas like the one that separates Alaska from Siberia dried, allowing now-extinct ancestors of lions, tigers, camels and elephants to cross over into North America. Some experts believe the first North Americans were hunters from Asia who crossed this ice-age "land bridge" in pursuit of game.

**The Value of Artifacts**
Artifacts are human-made objects that remind us of where we have come from and how our ancestors made their livelihoods. It is hard to imagine, but the earliest artifacts found in British Columbia—about twelve thousand years old—are from a time in the history of the world when dogs were the only domesticated animals, foodstuffs only grew wild and writing did not yet exist.

Others believe humans journeyed from Asia even earlier in boats or rafts. The oldest relics left behind by early occupants of BC—spear points found next to animal bones on the Queen Charlotte Islands—are about twelve thousand years old. Many First Nations cite oral traditions as evidence they were always in BC.

As the ice age ended, British Columbia's land mass took its present form, and human migrants adapted to the natural world we know today. These first British Columbians increased until their population peaked at somewhere between 80,000 and 200,000 before the next wave of newcomers began arriving from Europe in the late 1700s.

British Columbia's First Peoples were very sophisticated and produced masterful artwork, but they did not have written languages. Our understanding of the way they lived comes from ancient relics or artifacts they left behind, from languages and stories passed down through the generations, and from observations written down by early travellers from outside.

First Peoples spoke some thirty languages, each as distinct from the other as English is from German. Some of the languages had dialects, and most of them were part of larger language

Right: **A series of ancient rock paintings or pictographs in Kingcome Inlet depict ceremonial coppers, decorated plaques used in the important Kwakwa̱ka̱'wakw potlatch ceremony.** *Photo Jim Borrowman*

Below: **A weathered totem pole reposes in the grass at Gitwangak.** *Photo Chris Cheadle*

Previous pages: **'Ksan Historical Village and Museum at Hazelton is a cultural centre dedicated to illustrating the richness of the Gitx̱san culture and history.** *Photo Chris Cheadle*

families. Early attempts to render First Nations words into written English resulted in many mistakes about the names of different tribal groups. When the British explorer James Cook encountered the Nuu-chah-nulth people in 1778, he mistakenly thought they called themselves Nootka.

For two hundred years, all peoples on the west coast of Vancouver Island were referred to in official communications as Nootka, until the tribal council formally changed the name to Nuu-chah-nulth in 1980. In recent years many First Nations have replaced incorrect names given to them by early arrivals. Others, including the Sechelt, or Shishalh, are in the process of making changes. Still others such as the Haida are keeping the name as it is.

Across North America, First Peoples tended to concentrate along coastlines and river valleys where food, water and shelter were easiest to find. Among preferred locations in British Columbia were Vancouver Island, the Lower Mainland, Central Coast, Queen Charlotte Islands and major river valleys like the Fraser, Skeena and Columbia. About two-thirds of BC's First Peoples lived along or near the coast.

**The Tsimshian Annual Round**

Each group of First Peoples had its own distinctive yearly cycle. The Tsimshian of the Nass and Skeena river regions spent late winter and spring along the lower Nass River trading and fishing for oolichan, a small fish much prized for its oil. In late spring they moved to coastal islands to fish, hunt sea mammals and gather seaweed. Summer and fall were devoted to salmon fishing on the Skeena River as well as trading, hunting and gathering. In late fall the Tsimshian gathered at their winter villages to visit, dance and perform cultural rituals.

**This contemporary totem welcomes the thousands of visitors that brave the Capilano Suspension Bridge in North Vancouver each year.**

*Photo Rich Wheater*

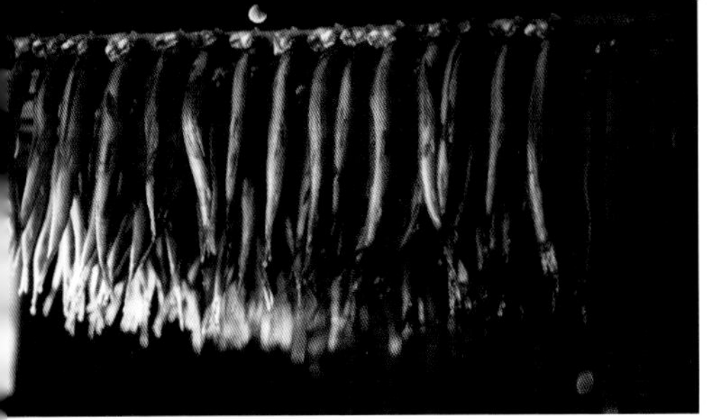

**Oolichan, a small smelt-like fish once abundant in coastal rivers, were harvested by First Nations and rendered for their rich oil, which was highly prized as a condiment.** *Photo Hans Grenander*

Coastal peoples divided the year into two parts. They spent the warmer months securing a livelihood. Their main source of food was salmon, which they fished and air-dried in large quantities to last through the year. Various parts of the red cedar tree were used for everything from baskets to clothing to houses to dugout canoes. They spent the cooler winter months indoors engaging in cultural and spiritual activities. Most coastal peoples lived in long wooden buildings housing perhaps thirty families. Each family had its own cooking hearth, work space, sleeping benches and storage area.

Above: **Moricetown Canyon on the Bulkley River has been a productive salmon-harvesting site of the Wet'suwet'en people for centuries.** *Photo Keith Douglas*

Right: **A Xeni Gwet'in elder dries fish in the Nemiah Valley. Salmon remains an important food source for many First Nations.** *Photo Vance Hanna*

Coastal peoples had complex societies based on inherited rank, wealth and intricate social conventions. At the heart of their rich ceremonial life lay the potlatch, a ceremony at which gifts were given to neighbouring groups to mark special occasions such as coming of age, marriage and the taking of leadership positions. The plentiful salmon runs and comparatively easy living conditions permitted coastal peoples to build up surplus material goods such as dried salmon, the grease of oolichans, dugout canoes and plates of native copper. The more of these items individuals were able to give away, the higher their status rose.

**Inside a Longhouse**

Emily Carr's 1899 verbal portrait of a longhouse interior at Ucluelet on the west coast of Vancouver Island echoes the sketch made a little over a century earlier by John Webber, a member of Captain James Cook's expedition: "Each of the large houses was the home of several families. The door and the smoke-hole were common to all, but each family had its own fire with its own things round it. That was their own home."

**Above:** *Image PDP00230 courtesy of Royal BC Museum, BC Archives*

**A Hamatsa dancer from the Kwakwaka'wakw First Nation performs at the Mungo Martin Longhouse in Victoria. The Hamatsa dancers are an exclusive Kwakwaka'wakw society.**

*Photo Chris Cheadle*

**A Nisga'a youth in ceremonial regalia and carved headdress.**
*Photo Chris Cheadle*

Leisure time also made artistic expression possible. Kin groups might have their own longhouses with the right to special ceremonies, sacred goods and designs, which sometimes took the form of carved ceremonial poles.

The harsher nature of British Columbia's interior meant that peoples living there spent more time obtaining food and shelter than their coastal counterparts and had less time to develop elaborate cultural activities. Hugh Brody described how "the Sekani became expert at the use of mountain resources; the Beaver specialized in the foothills and adjacent forests; the Slavey remained on the muskeg and along the river valleys of the Mackenzie drainage, where they made particularly extensive use of moose-hide boats in summer and snowshoes in winter." Fish was a dietary staple, usually supplemented by land animals and whatever else an austere habitat yielded.

**The Nisga'a of the Nass River Valley in northwestern British Columbia are organized into four clans. Here an elder of the Laxgibuu or wolf clan dons ceremonial regalia.**

*Photo Chris Cheadle*

**Decorated house fronts at 'Ksan Historical Village and Museum in Hazelton face the river waters, reflecting the design of traditional Gitxsan communities.**

*Photo Keith Douglas*

Above: **Old Gitxsan totem poles, preserved by the dry inland climate, still stand at the Skeena River village of Gitanyow (Kitwancool) in the Central Interior.** *Photo Chris Cheadle*

Living arrangements away from the coast tended to be simpler. Among interior Salish, circular pithouses with conical earth-covered roofs sheltered several families each winter; peoples to the north lived in dome-shaped lodges of poles and hides, which could easily be moved from place to place. Tribes were divided into small groups or bands, possibly no more than two or three families who moved about but lived together throughout the year. Interior peoples were generally less concerned with rank than their coastal counterparts.

**Living off the Land at Kitwancool**

British Columbia's First Peoples' close ties to the land have endured through the centuries. Emily Carr's description of a Gitxsan chief's family at Kitwancool enjoying "Indian ice cream" in 1928 could just as well have taken place before the coming of Europeans or in the twenty-first century. "One day after work I found the Douse family all sitting round the floor. In the centre of the group was Lizzie. She was beating something in a pail, beating it with her hands; her arms were blobbed with pink froth to the elbows. Everyone stuck his hand into Lizzie's pail and hooked out some of the froth in the crook of his fingers, then took delicious licks. They invited me to lick too. It was 'soperlallie,' or soap berry. It grows in the woods; when you beat the berry it froths up and has a queer bitter taste."

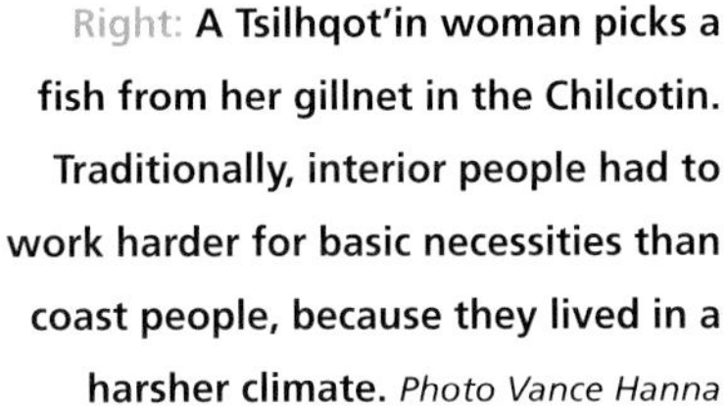

Right: **A Tsilhqot'in woman picks a fish from her gillnet in the Chilcotin. Traditionally, interior people had to work harder for basic necessities than coast people, because they lived in a harsher climate.** *Photo Vance Hanna*

Opposite: **A cluster of modern tipis occupies a grassy bench over the Fraser River outside Clinton. Tipis were used as summer lodges by the Shuswap First Nation.** *Photo Chris Harris*

**Siwash Rock, one of BC's most recognizable landmarks, as seen from the Stanley Park seawall, Vancouver.**
*Photo Ron Erwin*

**The Origins of Siwash Rock**

Squamish stories about the origins of Siwash Rock, a striking rocky spire that rises out of the sea near the western edge of Vancouver's Stanley Park, show how cultural knowledge passed down through the generations. According to Chillahminst, born about 1870, Siwash Rock represents a fisherman turned "into rock so people see not much good to be too smart." Qoitochetahl, born two decades later, explained that "the big hole in the nearby cliff is where the standing-up fisherman keeps his tackle." An early Vancouver resident recalled that when he was young, his First Nations counterparts gave Siwash Rock a wide berth for fear of being ensnared by its ghost.

Complex trading relations often developed between different groups, leading to surprisingly varied local economies. Through interpreters and middlemen, people exchanged such items as mountain-goat skins for abalone shells, and lichen dyes for dried seaweed. Over fifty kinds of trade goods and twenty separate trade routes were in use by 1750 by the ten thousand Tsimshian living near present-day Prince Rupert. Rivalry over control of trade goods and routes sometimes erupted into conflict and open warfare.

Wherever First Peoples lived across British Columbia, they shared a relationship to the natural environment and to the land. Supernatural beings pervaded the natural world, and both animate and inanimate beings were held to possess spirits whose power could either confer blessings or bring disaster. The past and present flowed together into a seamless web of being. All aspects of life, from rites of passage to everyday activity, encompassed an element of ritual and respect.

Right: **Potlatch guests assemble their canoes at the Kwakwa̱ka̱'wakw village of Tsaxis near Fort Rupert.**
*Painting by Bill Holm*

**A member of the Tsleil-Waututh Nation on Burrard Inlet, Chief Dan George became a film star and an eloquent First Nations spokesman.** *Painting by John Crittenden*

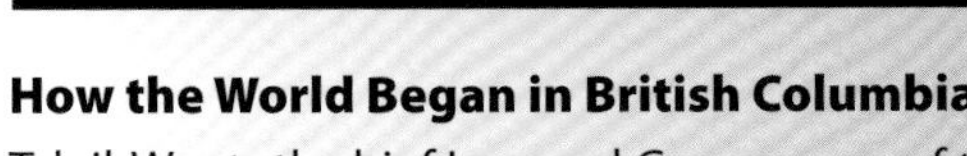

## How the World Began in British Columbia

Tsleil-Waututh chief Leonard George, son of the famed actor and orator Chief Dan George, has shared the story of how the world began in British Columbia. The story came down to him through his aunt's Squamish-speaking grandmother.

"It was the dawn of creation and all the world was new. The Creator was putting his final touches on Mother Earth. With this, Childman was born, my first grandfather.

"From time to time he would go to a high bluff to talk with the Creator. By and large he was content with his life, until he discovered that there was no one else like him. No one with his looks or his skin. No one who understood his language. One evening he went to his bluff to ask the Creator why, and as he stood there he was filled with a great inspiration to leap.

"Down through the air he went, and when his body broke the surface of the water, he plunged toward the ocean floor. Reaching the bottom, he filled his hands with sediment and seaweed and shells and set off for the surface. Exhausted, he swam to a sandy cove. The sun was setting, and without understanding why, he carefully cleared a large circle to the east. He put the sediment into the centre. The next day at first light he awoke to find a gift from the womb of Mother Earth, a woman, my first grandmother."

The lesson of the story, Leonard George said, is that his people "originated right here in British Columbia, and were not merely a branch of some other people."

**A face carved into a spruce tree marks the entrance to an old First Nations trail, Woss Lake on northern Vancouver Island. Aboriginal peoples' traditions hold that they have always lived in BC.** *Photo Chris Cheadle*

Opposite top: **The *Santiago*, a Spanish frigate under Juan Perez, made the first recorded contact between Europeans and aboriginal peoples of the future BC off Haida Gwaii on July 19, 1774.** *Painting by Gordon Miller*

Below: **First Nations women played a major role in traditional food gathering. Except for barren and inaccessible areas, every part of the province was occupied. Painting by William Hind.** *McCord Museum M607*

Indigenous people viewed land ownership differently from Europeans. While tribal territory was defended from outsiders, it was held in common by members of the tribe. Specific areas known for good fishing, hunting or berry picking might be reserved for individual family groups, however. To the present day many families have their own fishing stations in the Fraser Canyon and elsewhere in British Columbia.

Over the twelve thousand years or more that British Columbia's First Peoples occupied the land, they developed a sustainable way of life independent of any outside relations. The intrusions that began in the late 1700s resulted from European expansion, not from indigenous needs. Russia had recently established itself in present-day Alaska to the north, and Spain had occupied Mexico to the south for over two centuries. While the Russians stayed put, the Spanish were curious and mounted three expeditions up the west coast between 1774 and 1779. In doing so, they nominally claimed British Columbia for Spain.

Unknown artist, image A-00618 courtesy of Royal BC Museum, BC Archives

**Taking Possession of British Columbia**

The Spanish method for claiming territory was to put up wooden crosses along the shore, a tactic that did not take local people into account. As soon as a cross was erected in 1775 at 57°N, halfway up today's Alaska Panhandle, local people took it down and moved it closer to their dwellings. Captain Juan Francisco de la Bodega y Quadra noted hopefully in his journal that "they made us signs with their arms giving us to understand that they would keep it there." It is unlikely the locals understood that the white men hoped, by this simple means, to take possession of the lands they had occupied since time immemorial.

The British arrived at about the same time in search of the Northwest Passage, a mythical sea route across North America. They hoped it would expedite their lucrative trade with Asia, which depended on long sea routes around the southern extremities of Africa or South America. After explorations from eastern North America failed to turn up anything, the English national hero, Captain James Cook, was dispatched to find a route opening inland from the Pacific Ocean. First anchoring at Nootka Sound on the west coast of Vancouver Island in the spring of 1778, he sailed north along the coast before turning away toward Asia. Although Cook put an end to British dreams of a shortcut to Asia, his voyage had two important consequences.

**Female Fur Traders**

Nootka Sound on the west coast of Vancouver Island was the favoured stop for early explorers and traders, who often found themselves facing local Nuu-chah-nulth women when it came to the business of the visit, trading for sea-otter pelts. These female fur traders proved to be harder bargainers than the men. As one trader complained, "I dreaded the sight of a Woman, for whenever any were present, they were sure to Preside over & direct all commercial transactions, and as often as that was the case, I was obliged to pay three times the Price."

Above: **Photo by Edward Curtis.** *Image D-08313 courtesy of Royal BC Museum, BC Archives*

Opposite: **Friendly Cove in Nootka Sound was the site of the first prolonged contact between indigenous people and Europeans.** *Photo Jeremy Koreski*

Above: **Charles Jeffreys' painting of Captain James Cook's meeting with First Nations at Nootka Sound. Cook's expedition triggered BC's first economic boom.** *Imperial Oil Collection series, Library and Archives Canada, accession no.1972-26-765, item 00765, C-073721*

**Two Nuu-chah-nulth painted by Jacques Grasset de Saint-Sauveur, 1757–1810. Early traders found First Nations people eager to participate in economic activities.** *Images PDP02030 and PDP02031 courtesy of Royal BC Museum, BC Archives*

The first consequence of Cook's expedition was to trigger British Columbia's first economic boom. Coastal people wore attractive robes made from the fur of the sea otter, a small marine mammal abundant along the outer shores of Vancouver Island. Cook's crew acquired a small stock of these luxuriant pelts for paltry sums. Stopping in China on their way home, they were able to sell the furs for much higher prices. Word got out about the profits to be made trading sea-otter pelts, and in 1785 English sea captain James Hanna made the first voyage to trade furs between Nootka and China.

A maritime fur trade quickly developed in which New England merchants from the newly independent United States soon beat out their competitors. First Nations people did the hunting in exchange for trade goods that included iron utensils, guns and alcohol. Over 170 separate ships from several countries traded along the Pacific Northwest coast extending south through present-day Oregon during the peak years of exploitation between 1785 and 1825, by which time the sea otter was all but wiped out.

The second consequence of Cook's visit was a dispute between Britain and Spain over control of Nootka Sound, perceived as the gateway to the Pacific Northwest. Each country sought to

Frances Barkley, the first European woman known to have reached the BC coast, was only seventeen years old when she joined her husband, Capt. Charles W. Barkley, on the trading ship ***Imperial Eagle***. *Painting by Steve Mayo*

support its claim by acquiring as much information as possible. In the process Captain George Vancouver and his Spanish counterpart Juan Francisco de la Bodega y Quadra mapped much of the coast. A diplomatic resolution of 1790–94 gave trading rights to both countries without determining ownership. Spain turned its attention elsewhere, and in 1819 gave up all claim.

**A Warm Squamish Welcome**

In the spring of 1792, when Captain George Vancouver visited Burrard Inlet, the site of the future metropolis that would bear his name, the Squamish welcomed him and his men to their territory. Vancouver described in his journal how his vessels were "met by about fifty Indians, in their canoes, who conducted themselves with the greatest decorum and civility, presenting us with several fish … resembling the smelt." The Squamish were being resourceful, keen to trade for goods they did not possess. "These good people, finding we were inclined to make some return for their hospitality, shewed much understanding in preferring iron to copper." The Squamish were naturally curious about these strange intruders, so unlike anything of their own world. Vancouver noted that they "examined the color of our skins with infinite curiosity."

Along with their Musqueam neighbours, the Squamish are still very much part of Metro Vancouver.

**British Columbia's First Female Visitors**

The first white woman known to have set eyes on BC and the first non-white woman from outside the region arrived together in 1787. Frances Barkley was the seventeen-year-old bride of a sea captain in search of sea-otter pelts. Winee was her young Hawaiian maidservant, hired during a stop at the islands. Winee survives in a contemporary image, and Frances through a story passed down in her family. As relations between sailors and aboriginals visiting on-board ship reached a tense point, Frances is said to have emerged from her cabin with her long red-gold hair blowing in the breeze, whereupon the visitors fell back in awe, convinced such a vision must be supernatural.

**Above:** *Sketch of Winee from John Meares,* Voyages Made in the Years 1788–89, *published 1795.*

The future British Columbia faced east as well as west. Land-based fur traders of the North West Company in Montreal sought to establish western trade ahead of their competitors in the London-based Hudson's Bay Company. In 1793 Alexander Mackenzie travelled by interior rivers and First Nations trading routes to the ocean near today's Bella Coola. This made him the first person of European ancestry known to lead an overland crossing of North America north of Mexico. In 1808 his business partner Simon Fraser reached the mouth of the river that would bear his name. About the same time David Thompson, another Nor'wester, travelled down the Columbia River to explore areas to the south.

**The land-based fur trade was built on the backs of "voyageurs," labourers mostly of mixed French-Canadian and aboriginal ancestry.** *Frances Anne Hopkins, Library and Archives Canada, accession no. 189-401-3, C-002773*

### Overland to the Pacific Ocean

Travelling overland by canoe and on foot, fur trader Alexander Mackenzie reached the Pacific Ocean at the mouth of the Bella Coola River in July 1793. To mark the feat he "mixed up some vermilion in melted grease and inscribed, in large characters, on the southeast face of the rock on which we had slept last night, this brief memorial—'Alexander Mackenzie, from Canada, by land, the twenty-second of July, one thousand seven hundred and ninety-three.'"

Above left: ***Shooting the Rapids*** **by Frances Anne Hopkins. Agents of European expansion, the voyageurs criss-crossed the continent using canoes made of birchbark.**

*Frances Anne Hopkins, Library and Archives Canada, accession no. 189-401-3, C-002774*

Above: **The explorers who produced the first maps of what is today BC became known as "discoverers," but they could not have done so without their aboriginal guides.** *Frances Anne Hopkins, Library and Archives Canada, accession no. 189-401-3, C-002771*

Right: **Painting of Simon Fraser.** *Unknown artist, image PDP02258 courtesy of Royal BC Museum, BC Archives*

Opposite: **The sun sets on Our Lady of Good Hope Catholic Church in Fort St. James, built in 1873. Fort St. James was founded in 1806 by Simon Fraser.** *Photo Chris Jaksa*

### Crossing British Columbia

The first fur traders to cross the British Columbian mainland would have been swallowed up by the sprawling, unmapped wilderness and never seen again but for the crucial assistance of local men and women. Alexander Mackenzie noted repeatedly in his journal that "without Indians I have very little hope of succeeding." A Dakelh assured Mackenzie that "the way is so often travelled by them that their path is visible throughout the whole journey," a claim he found accurate as he made his way to the coast. Fifteen years later fellow trader Simon Fraser wrote in his journal, "I have been for a long period among the Rocky Mountains, but have never seen anything equal to this country . . . We had to pass where no human being should venture. Yet in those places there is a regular footpath impressed, or rather indented by frequent travelling upon the very rocks."

Above: **The fur trade was British Columbia's main economic driver for half a century.** *Photo Jim Jurica*

Below: **Fort Langley, now open to visitors, was a major fur-trade centre on the lower Fraser River.** *Photo Gary Fiegehen*

In the course of these explorations, Europeans established small fur-trading posts that strengthened Britain's claim to the region. The agreement ending the War of 1812 between Britain and the United States established a loose joint occupation of the Pacific Northwest. The large area did not much interest either country, apart from the immediate economic advantages of trading for pelts.

In the early nineteenth century, land-based fur trade developed across the Central Interior of British Columbia extending south to the Columbia River. In 1821 the Hudson's Bay Company took over the North West Company and thereafter managed the trade through two departments, New Caledonia to the north and Columbia to the south. Forts St. James, Langley and Kamloops were among the posts where employees lived year-round while trading with local peoples for pelts. Overall this trade was a relatively minor intrusion into First Nations' lives. Local peoples decided if and when they wanted to trade. New goods entered local economies but, for the most part, lives continued much as before.

The fundamental shift for indigenous peoples came when Europeans decided to stay and compete for land and resources rather than merely trading and moving on. This transition began in earnest in Oregon during the 1830s as Americans headed west to form settlements. They did so in such growing numbers that the Hudson's Bay Company decided, in order to ensure its future well-being, to establish a new post on Vancouver Island to the north.

Fort Victoria was constructed in 1843 under the supervision of fur trader James Douglas. Growing agitation by American settlers caused the United States and Britain to sign the Treaty of Washington in 1846. The treaty handed the present-day states of Washington, Idaho and Oregon to the United States and extended the international boundary west along the 49th parallel from the Rocky Mountains to tidewater before looping around the southern tip of Vancouver Island.

***The Return of a War Party*** **by Paul Kane, painted 1847, shows Fort Victoria with the Songhees village in the background.** *With permission of the Royal Ontario Museum © ROM*

**An Important Fur-Trade Intermediary**

Although there are stories of indigenous peoples being awestruck by the strange appearance and impressive possessions of the Europeans at first meeting, it is remarkable how quickly many adapted and met the new challenge head-on. The Dakelh chief Kwah, who lived near Fort St. James between 1755 and 1840, was indispensable in securing the many thousands of salmon needed annually to feed traders stationed across New Caledonia. As one of the traders noted, Kwah was "the only Indian who can and Will give fish, and on whom we Must depend in great Measure. It behooves us to endeavour to Keep friends with him." For his part, Kwah demanded respect: "Do not I manage my affairs as well as you do yours?" he once protested to trader Daniel Harmon. "When did you ever hear that [Kwah] was in danger of starving? … I never want for anything, and my family is always well-clothed." In his refusal to be daunted by the Europeans, Kwah was typical of many aboriginal leaders of his generation.

**Native people were crucial fur-trade intermediaries, as shown in this painting of First Nations at Victoria gorge by William Hind, 1860.**

*Image PDP02611 courtesy of Royal BC Museum, BC Archives*

Nanaimo's famous bastion is an authentic relic of the old Hudson's Bay Company fort. According to a legend, a Snuneymuxw elder known as the Coal Tyee showed traders the area's rich coal deposits. *Courtesy of the Nanaimo Community Archives, Photograph No. 1993 047 A-PCI*

The Treaty of Washington not only gave the future British Columbia its southern boundary, it ceded that territory to Britain. In 1849 Britain made Vancouver Island a British colony and sent the gentleman adventurer Richard Blanshard out from London as unpaid governor, but that was about all. Britain was not much interested in this remote corner of North America, and handed over everyday administration of its new possession to the Hudson's Bay Company for ten years on the condition that it encourage colonization.

Upon Blanshard's unhappy departure in 1850, James Douglas took on the additional responsibility of governor, which ensured that the links would remain close between colony and fur trade. In practice, Douglas recognized, "the interests of the Colony, and the Fur Trade will never harmonize." Colonization, rather than being encouraged, was kept to the minimum needed to keep the British government from revoking the agreement. Some retired fur traders did settle down around Fort Victoria, which had a white population in 1855 of 200 with another 350 living in outlying areas.

A second small community of settlers emerged on Vancouver Island when the Hudson's Bay Company began developing the rich coal deposits at Nanaimo. Demand for coal by steam-driven vessels along the coast created a growing market, and some two dozen miners and their families were brought out from England. By 1855 Nanaimo had about 150 whites.

England's lack of interest in its fledgling colony meant that it gave little attention to making treaties with indigenous people to acquire land for settlement. Douglas negotiated fourteen small treaties covering the area around Victoria and the coal mines in the years 1850–54, but thereafter lacked the funds to do more. Britain showed a brief interest in Vancouver Island with the outbreak of the Crimean War in Europe in 1854, and the Royal Navy began to dock ships at Esquimalt, just west of Fort Victoria. All the same, Vancouver Island's European population barely exceeded seven hundred, with handfuls stationed at the various fur trade posts scattered across the mainland. Newcomers were outnumbered by their indigenous neighbours by as much as fifty to one.

**The Fragile British Colony of Vancouver Island**

Proclaimed in 1849, Vancouver Island was a British colony in name only. Governor James Douglas's son-in-law, J.S. Helmcken, considered that few places "have been so solitary—so free from intercourse." Its chief administrator only worked part-time, it had virtually no civic budget, and its main economic engine, the fur trade, was in decline. Without a change in fortunes, it seemed fated to wither away, or fall to the growing American presence in the region.

Above: **Restored room at Craigflower Manor, Victoria. The Hudson's Bay Company had a mandate to encourage permanent British settlements, of which Craigflower was a rare example.** *Photo Chris Cheadle*

# 3

# The Making of British Columbia

If the gold rush had not begun in 1858, today's British Columbia might never have come into being. Britain's enthusiasm for its farthest-flung possession declined alongside the diminishing revenues of the fur trade while American settlement kept increasing south of the border. Many believed it was only a matter of time until the United States extended its reach north to Alaska.

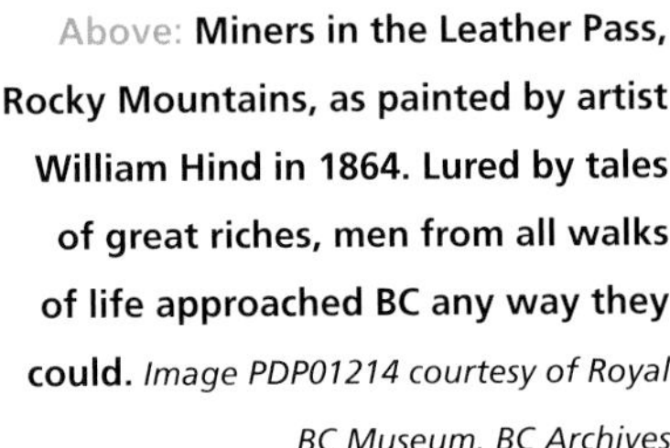

Above: **Miners in the Leather Pass, Rocky Mountains, as painted by artist William Hind in 1864. Lured by tales of great riches, men from all walks of life approached BC any way they could.** *Image PDP01214 courtesy of Royal BC Museum, BC Archives*

Top right: **Few female faces were to be seen among the gold rushers who gathered in the BC interior. Painting by William Hind.** *Image PDP00032 courtesy of Royal BC Museum, BC Archives*

Right: **The gold rush transformed Victoria from a quiet trading post to a bustling boom town. Fort Victoria was painted by Sarah Crease on September 25, 1860.** *Image PDP02892 courtesy of Royal BC Museum, BC Archives*

Previous pages: **All anyone needed was a 50-cent gold pan and a hardy constitution to have a chance at making a fortune during the BC gold rush. William Hind did this famous painting of a typical miner circa 1864.** *Image PDP02612 courtesy of Royal BC Museum, BC Archives*

**Businessman and community leader Mifflin Westal Gibbs was one of many American blacks who followed the gold rush to Victoria in 1858 to escape racial discrimination prevalent in the US.** *Image B-01601 courtesy of Royal BC Museum, BC Archives*

There matters stood until news leaked out about the discovery of gold in Fraser River sandbars. Nearby California, recently acquired by the United States from Mexico, had been transformed by a huge gold rush, beginning in 1849. British Columbia offered a new opportunity and many miners were ready to move north. The first arrivals in the spring of 1858 were mostly experienced miners from California. As news spread, others came from farther away, including British North America—the future Canada—Great Britain and China. Among the newcomers was a contingent of Californian blacks seeking to escape racial discrimination in the United States.

Fort Victoria became a bustling emporium. Most men landed at Esquimalt just next door. While the vast majority came to get rich quick, a few were more resourceful. They were San Francisco merchants who brought the goods needed to set up shop and soon did a roaring business. Within six weeks more than two hundred buildings went up. The first large merchant house to compete with the Hudson's Bay Company was started by two American blacks, Peter Lester and Mifflin Gibbs.

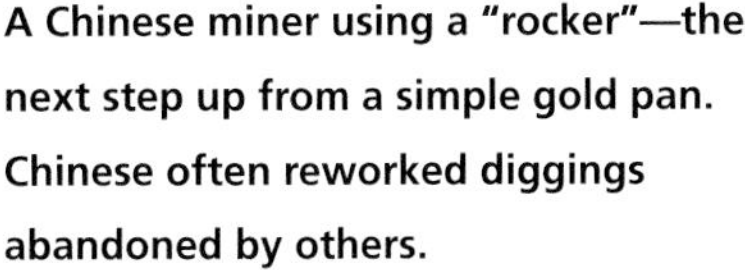

**A Chinese miner using a "rocker"—the next step up from a simple gold pan. Chinese often reworked diggings abandoned by others.** *McCord Museum MP-1993.6.10.13*

### Gold Fever

The lure of gold came from its physical appearance, its scarcity and the apparent ease with which single individuals could extract the metal. To go from rags to riches overnight, it was only necessary to reach the latest finds, stake a claim and scoop up the precious metal. Men became addicted. One veteran wrote to his family on the eve of the British Columbia gold rush in 1858, "I have spent the best portion of my life in chasing after gold which has unfitted me for any other occupation, and to throw away the present chance appears to me like sacrificing all my past years of toil."

**Getting to the Goldfields**

Before the Cariboo Wagon Road, there was no easy way to get to the goldfields. Most men landed at Esquimalt near Victoria, secured a mining licence and supplies, and headed out. While a lucky few secured passage across the Strait of Georgia on the Hudson's Bay steamer, others bought dugout canoes or constructed rafts. One prospective miner mused about the Fraser River leading from the Strait of Georgia to the goldfields, "Will the number ever be known of those who met death in that dangerous river or on its inhospitable shores?"

The men travelled as far as water could take them, then made their way through unmarked terrain characterized by dense forest, sharp inclines and rocky precipices. "We soon found ourselves in the quandary of not knowing where to go; one advised one thing, one another and a third another, all equally certain to be 'a dead thing,' until we were fairly puzzled." Getting to the goldfields meant a hard slog and ever-present danger.

**Above:** *Henry James Warre, Library and Archives of Canada, accession number 1965-76-41, item 00041, C027586K*

Gold seekers are incredibly audacious. Men endured great hardships in the hopes of being the lucky ones to get rich quick. Some estimates put the total reaching British Columbia in 1858 at thirty thousand, followed by thousands more arriving by sea and overland during the next half-dozen years of the gold rush. Most soon left, for the difficulties of getting to the finds were enormous, especially as miners found gold farther north in the Cariboo. By 1864 rough trails had been replaced by the Cariboo Wagon Road, an ambitious and ruinously expensive project that ended at the boom town of Barkerville.

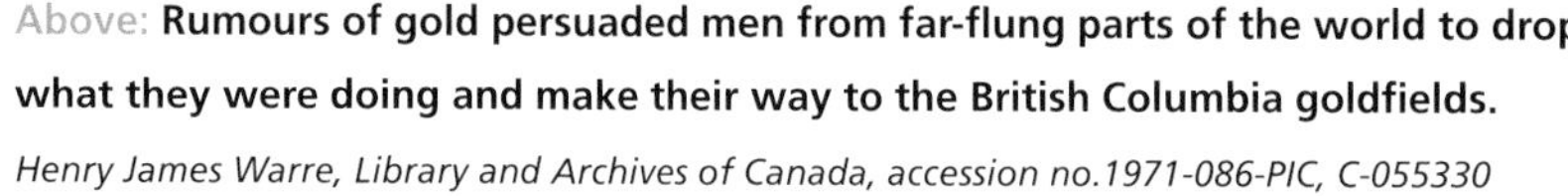

Above: **Rumours of gold persuaded men from far-flung parts of the world to drop what they were doing and make their way to the British Columbia goldfields.** *Henry James Warre, Library and Archives of Canada, accession no.1971-086-PIC, C-055330*

Top: **The 650-kilometre (400-mile) Cariboo Wagon Road, built with pickaxes and shovels, made the BC interior accessible by stagecoach.** *Edward Roper, Peter Winkworth Collection, Library and Archives of Canada, accession no. R9266-549, item 00549, C150726 (E000756685)*

The gold rush forced Britain's hand. But first, it forced the hand of Governor Douglas. The mainland was under invasion by unruly Americans. A miner described Yale at the entrance to the Fraser Canyon as "a city of tents and shacks, stores, barrooms and gambling houses" where "miners, prospectors, traders, gamblers and painted ladies mingled in the throng." Douglas was only the governor of Vancouver Island, and had no formal authority over the mainland, but rather than wait the months needed for authorization by London and risk a US takeover, he acted on his own to assert control over the goldfields and required all miners to obtain licences. It was his finest hour. He managed to bluff his way until August 2, 1858, when Britain formally declared the mainland a separate colony and made him governor. Queen Victoria personally christened the new colony British Columbia.

**How British Columbia Got Its Name**

Once Britain declared a second British colony on the mainland, it had to find a name. The French had already given the name New Caledonia to some islands in the Pacific, so Britain abandoned that possibility. The second choice of Columbia—honouring the other Hudson's Bay department that centred on the Columbia River—could be confused with a region of South America. Queen Victoria made the decision by tacking "British" on to Columbia.

Above: **James Douglas acted decisively in meeting the challenge of the gold rush, laying firm foundations for the province that was to be.**

*Unknown artist, image PDP00090 courtesy of Royal BC Museum, BC Archives*

Left: **Paddlewheelers similar to the *Paystreak* carried miners and their supplies as far inland as the boom town of Yale on the lower Fraser.**

*Painting by John Horton*

**Chinese Gold Miners**
From 1858 onwards, Chinese miners arrived from San Francisco and directly from China, often wearing traditional dress and a queue (pigtail) that showed deference to their emperor. They carried their belongings on a pole slung over their shoulders, with clothing, blankets and mining equipment on one end and supplies and cooking utensils on the other. Their appearance set them apart, but so did their tenacity. A fellow miner described how "this much-enduring and industrious race are generally to be found in little clusters, at work upon diggings deserted by the whites." A minority of the four thousand or more Chinese in British Columbia at the height of the gold rush were merchants competing for business in Victoria and elsewhere, some of them very successfully.

**Above: Painting by William Hind.**
*McCord Museum M609*

In exchange for being made governor of both colonies, Douglas severed his ties with the fur trade, which in any case had lost its dominance. Following the discovery of gold in the far Northwest, Britain asserted the mainland colony's sovereignty north to 60° and east to the 120th meridian, essentially putting in place the province's present boundaries.

The Royal Engineers, a detachment of soldiers specializing in infrastructure, were dispatched from Britain to build roads and select a capital. Initially it was located at Fort Langley, where the new colony was proclaimed on November 19, 1858. The weather ensured that this propitious event was distinctly British Columbian. "Yesterday, the birthday of British Columbia, was ushered in by a steady rain, which continued perseveringly throughout the whole day." Fort Langley soon lost out to a site nearer the mouth of the Fraser River, which the head of the

Royal Engineers, Colonel Richard Moody, considered easier to defend against a possible invasion. The new capital was named New Westminster for the British original.

By their very nature, gold rushes have limited life spans. By the mid-1860s British Columbia's gold rush was in decline, and the white population was falling. So were government revenues, which in no way could pay off the large debt left by the construction of the Cariboo Wagon Road. To save money, and much to the dismay of Vancouver Island residents, Britain folded their colony into its younger mainland counterpart in 1866.

**British Columbia's Francophone Community**

Francophones were among the first non-aboriginal people in BC. Six French Canadians accompanied Alexander Mackenzie on his 1793 trek across the Rocky Mountains to the Pacific Ocean. French-Canadian voyageurs were also part of the expeditions of Simon Fraser (among them Jules-Maurice Quesnel, namesake of the modern city) and David Thompson. In 1827 sixteen French Canadians travelled with James McMillan north from Fort Vancouver on the Columbia River to the lower Fraser River, where they established Fort Langley. By 1850, a total of eight hundred French Canadians had worked west of the Rockies in the fur trade and some of them had taken up permanent residence. In 1851 a military corps was established to protect Fort Victoria. Called the Voltigeurs, it consisted largely of francophones.

The Fraser River gold rush attracted more francophones to BC, not only from Quebec but from France as well. There were enough French-speaking people in Victoria by 1858 to warrant the appearance of a French newspaper, *Le Courrier de la Nouvelle Calédonie*. The Roman Catholic Church, under the leadership of Bishop Modeste Demers, played an important role in bringing French culture to BC. The Sisters of St. Ann established a school in Victoria as early as 1858 and then others across BC. Construction of the CPR attracted French-Canadian workers to the province; some of them later became farmers in the Fraser Valley at Hatzic Prairie, which remained a French-speaking centre until World War I.

The francophone presence was also felt elsewhere. In 1909 the Fraser Mills Lumber Company near New Westminster brought forty families from Quebec to replace its Asian workforce. The families were provided with a school and a church, Notre Dame de Lourdes, and by 1913 the small community of Maillardville had emerged. A francophone community developed in Vancouver following World War II, centred around the Blessed Sacrament Church. Francophones continue to play an important role in British Columbian life.

Opposite: **Fort Langley, an HBC post built on the banks of the Fraser in 1827, was an important stop for miners before departing for the goldfields of the interior. BC was declared a colony here on November 19, 1858. Painting by William Henry Newton.**

*Image PDP00029 courtesy of Royal BC Museum, BC Archives*

Above: **The Royal Navy ship HMS *Cameleon*, in 1870 with crew aboard the poop deck.** *Image B-01508 courtesy of Royal BC Museum, BC Archives*

The long-term status of the United Colony of British Columbia provoked much debate. The contingent allied with Britain favoured the existing situation, whereas arrivals from within British North America preferred joining the new Canadian Confederation, created in 1867.

Others sought annexation to the United States. American aspirations had briefly erupted into war in 1859 over jurisdiction of San Juan Island near Victoria. The day after Britain confirmed the Canadian Confederation, the United States purchased Alaska from Russia, which renewed interest in acquiring British Columbia as well.

Britain may have been momentarily tempted to give in to American demands. At the time of the Alaska sale, Britain was negotiating with the United States over reparations for having permitted the South to build warships on British territory during the recently concluded Civil War. The US secretary of state proposed to take British Columbia in settlement. The British demurred, not out of love for its remote colony but because the Royal Navy, the power behind the British Empire, had recently moved its Pacific headquarters from Valparaiso, Chile, to Esquimalt. To give up British Columbia would inconvenience the Royal Navy. In 1869, following a visit to Victoria by the American secretary of state, a hundred Victoria residents, many of them merchants from California, submitted two petitions to Congress requesting annexation. This caused a flutter, but no action ensued and the surge abated.

Below: **In 1865 the Royal Navy moved its headquarters from Valparaiso to Esquimalt, giving Britain a reason for protecting the territory from US incursion. Painting by Alexander Rattray.** *Image PDP00183 courtesy of Royal BC Museum, BC Archives*

Britain meanwhile stepped into the breach. It was interested in colonies only so far as they benefited the mother country economically, and a struggling British Columbia seemed unlikely ever to do this. From Britain's perspective, the best course lay in unloading the remote possession on the newly formed Dominion of Canada (consisting of Nova Scotia, New Brunswick and parts of present-day Quebec and Ontario). The handful of men dominating British Columbian politics had to be convinced that union was the best option, and in 1869 Britain appointed a new governor, Anthony Musgrave, charged with precisely that task. He cajoled the colonial legislature into supporting a formal proposal to join Canada by setting out conditions the local politicians considered so extreme they would likely be rejected. Not only did they stipulate that Canada must take over the colony's crippling debt, they demanded it build a wagon road all the way from central Canada to the west coast. The province sent a three-man delegation to Ottawa prepared to put up a fight.

British Columbia's demands were received in Ottawa as being quite reasonable. The wagon road was even upgraded to a railway to be completed within a decade. The delegation had no choice but to accept the terms of union, and on July 1, 1871, British Columbia joined the Canadian Confederation.

Above: **Fisgard Lighthouse at the entrance to Esquimalt Harbour was BC's first manned light when it was built in 1860.** *Photo David Nunuk*

Below: **BC's first parliamentary government after joining Confederation was made up exclusively of property-owning male subjects and headed by John McCreight, the first premier.** *Image A-04737 courtesy of Royal BC Museum, BC Archives*

**British Columbia's Very Own Language**

Early traders soon realized they would never be able to learn all the languages spoken by indigenous peoples across the Pacific Northwest, so they made up a simple language everybody could understand. It was called Chinook because it was partly based on the Pacific Northwest's most widely known aboriginal language, that of the Chinook people of the lower Columbia River. The Chinook jargon possesses at most seven hundred words derived in approximately equal proportions from the Chinook language, from the Nuu-chah-nulth people of Vancouver Island, from French and English and from imitated sounds (*Wa-wa* means talk, *hee-hee* means laugh; *lip-lip* means boil, *chick-chick* means wagon). For a time, Chinook was likely spoken by more British Columbians than any other single tongue, including English. Between 1891 and 1904 a Kamloops missionary, Father Le Jeune, published a widely circulated Chinook jargon newspaper, the *Wawa.* Many industries employing a mix of people speaking different languages relied on Chinook into the mid-twentieth century.

**Above: Painting by Emily Carr.** *Image PDP02159 courtesy of Royal BC Museum, BC Archives*

Shortly thereafter, elections chose the six members of the federal Parliament (MPs) allotted to British Columbia and the twenty-five members of the new provincial legislative assembly (MLAs). The province's population was minute. It consisted in 1870 of about 8,500 whites, 1,500 Chinese, 500 blacks and an uncertain number of indigenous people. Diseases brought by Europeans, including a devastating smallpox epidemic in 1862–63, had reduced the aboriginal population to perhaps 25,000, at most 40,000. The right to vote was restricted to literate males aged twenty-one or over, resident for six months, who were Canadian-born or naturalized British subjects and held a certain amount of property. The preponderance of men over women in the immigrant population, due to the masculine character of the fur trade and gold rush, meant that 3,800 men nonetheless voted in the first provincial election. The man selected as BC's first premier, John McCreight, was not the leader of the political party electing the most candidates, since there were no parties, but rather the head of the largest shifting coalition of like-minded persons. This pattern would continue for the rest of the nineteenth century.

Based in Victoria, the provincial government was a fairly passive affair, apart from dispensing patronage and encouraging resource exploitation. It enacted free elementary schooling in 1872, but offered little else in the way of social services.

Entry into Confederation greatly changed the position of indigenous peoples. Under the terms of union, as set out in the British North America Act, responsibility for Indians transferred to the Dominion government, which unfortunately committed many of the same kind of errors

as did most other colonial governments of the time. It would take almost a century before aboriginal people in BC achieved respect as equal citizens with the right to pursue their own cultural traditions. Only then did they cease to be viewed as obstacles to settlement to be moved out of the way onto reserves or integrated into white society as quickly as possible.

With one exception, no more treaties were signed in British Columbia after the first fourteen that Douglas had struck on Vancouver Island in the early 1850s. Treaty No. 8 signed in 1899 with First Nations on the prairies included the Northeast region due to its location east of the Rocky Mountains.

**Early Schooling**

The only social service for which the new province took responsibility was free elementary schooling. Parents most often took the initiative by erecting a schoolhouse, usually quite primitive, and then securing a teacher. Up to 1900, when BC acquired its first teacher training college, teachers only had to pass a test of general knowledge. Women who took up teaching usually only did it for a few years prior to marriage, while men typically taught just long enough to get into some better-paying line of work.

**Above:** *Photo courtesy Nicola Valley Museum Archives*

Left: **When BC joined Canada, responsibility for First Nations was passed over to the federal government.** *Image G-04397 courtesy of Royal BC Museum, BC Archives*

Opposite: **The central structure of the original Legislative Buildings in Victoria, known as the "birdcages."** *Image A-00841 courtesy of Royal BC Museum, BC Archives*

Above: **For First Nations children, formal education was slow in coming. Painting by Emily Carr.**
*McCord Museum M22155*

**Schooling for Indian Children**

The federal government had responsibility for the education of Indians, as indigenous persons under its charge were called, but often chose to subsidize schools run by missionaries rather than open its own. While day schools operated on some reserves, the emphasis was on residential schools, where children would be separated from their families—and the old ways—for months and years on end. All instruction was in English, and children were prohibited from using their own languages.

By 1900 British Columbia had fourteen residential and twenty-eight day schools, enrolling some 40 percent of Indian children across the province. By the end of World War I most attended school for at least a year or two, but this achievement was misleading. Whereas virtually all pupils in provincial schools completed the elementary grades, the overwhelming majority of Indian children never got beyond grade one or two.

**Above:** *Image A-04485 courtesy of Royal BC Museum, BC Archives*

For white British Columbians, it was the promised rail line that mattered. As Governor Douglas's son-in-law Dr. Helmcken foretold during the Confederation debates, "The Colony had no love for Canada; the bargain for love could not be; it can only be the advancement of material interest which will lead to union." When rail construction was postponed for political and financial reasons, talk turned to seceding from Canada.

In 1878 Canadian Prime Minister John A. Macdonald launched a nation-building strategy he

CANADIAN PACIFIC

CANADIAN PACIFIC
THE EMPIRE'S GREATEST RAILWAY

Above: **During the fifteen-year wait for the promised railway from the east, some impatient west coasters mounted a secession movement.** *CPR Archives, A6399*

Left: **The arrival of the first passenger train in Gastown signalled the transformation of the small sawmill town of Granville in the city of Vancouver.** *City of Vancouver Archives, CAN P6 /A25312*

called the National Policy, which encouraged economic development through higher tariffs, immigration and a transcontinental railway. The National Policy echoed the imperialist sentiment of the day in viewing the role of the periphery—western Canada, for example—as strengthening the economy of the centre by providing raw materials that would return as manufactured goods.

Value added in the form of jobs and industrial growth accrued to the centre, in practice the two most populous provinces, Ontario and Quebec. The imposition of differential freight rates and tariffs on manufactured imports also made it difficult for the periphery to develop independently of the centre.

While detrimental to British Columbia over the long term, the National Policy got rail construction underway. The Montreal syndicate that won the right to build the Canadian Pacific Railway (CPR) received considerable government assistance, including large land grants. Labourers from China did much of the hard work, and over fifteen thousand entered through Victoria for that purpose. The syndicate, seeking to maximize profits by putting the western terminus at the location offering the best land, opted for the south shore of Burrard Inlet.

Left: *CPR Archives 6406*

**The Boldness of Rail Construction**

British Columbia's rugged terrain made rail construction a bold undertaking. Surveyors located the most feasible route in advance, then the crews had to zigzag up steep mountain grades, blast tunnels and build bridges over deep canyons. A young Maritimer travelling to BC shortly after the line's completion bragged to her sister, "I stood out on the platform when the train was rushing down the steepest grade on the line—whizzing past rocks & ravines & torrents—and it was the wind, and not scare that finally drove me in. . . . It was all fine, grand, sublime, terrific!!"

Above: **Following the arrival of the CPR in 1886, Vancouver quickly outgrew its milltown roots.**
*Image B-03657 courtesy of Royal BC Museum, BC Archives*

Top: **Building a cantilever rail bridge near Cisco Flat south of Lytton on the Fraser River, 1884.**
*Image D-08738 courtesy of Royal BC Museum, BC Archives*

Opposite: **The *Empress of India* docking in Vancouver, 1891. CPR's sleek "Empress" ocean liners linked Vancouver with Asia, presaging BC's role as a portal for Pacific Rim trade.**
*Bailey Bros. photo, Vancouver Public Library, VPL 19882*

The rail line transformed the small logging community at Gastown into the new city of Vancouver. Hundreds of new businesses led the way, as in Victoria in spring 1858. A bush fire that destroyed much of Vancouver in June 1886 did little to dampen enthusiasm. A visitor two years later counted "ever so many brick buildings in various stages of advancement." By 1891, Vancouver, with a southern boundary then extending only to present-day 16th Avenue, housed almost fourteen thousand people.

Britain lay just over two weeks away by steamship from Montreal, and very soon the CPR extended its reach from Vancouver west to Asia. The first of the sleek Empress liners went into service in 1891. What became known as the "all-red route"—red being the colour for the British Empire on maps of the time—linked Britain with her Asian and Australian colonies via British Columbia. In little more than a decade Vancouver replaced Victoria as the province's commercial centre and the principal port through which goods moved to world markets.

Stops along the new rail line quickly developed into substantial communities. Kamloops and Revelstoke became market towns for nearby miners, farmers and ranchers. Wherever the train stopped, travel continued by water. Sternwheelers operated on lakes and rivers throughout much of the interior, and steamships ran up and down the west coast.

**The Age of Sternwheelers**

Used since the early nineteenth century on the Mississippi River and in the California gold rush, sternwheelers seemed ideal for British Columbia's inland waterways. Flat-bottomed, with a draft of only fifteen to twenty centimetres (six to eight inches), sternwheelers bobbed like ducks on top of the water. Powered by a single paddlewheel at the stern, they needed no wharf. The bow simply nosed ashore while the stern remained in the water, and the ship needed only a plank walkway to unload and load cargo and passengers. "It can lie right in with its snout on the beach like a crocodile and back out again into deep water." The first sternwheelers ran during the gold rush. On the railway's completion, they became the vital link taking passengers as far as the water reached. About forty sternwheelers operated over time in British Columbia. The last sternwheeler, the venerable *Moyie*—now a historic site in Kaslo—quit running in 1957.

**Above:** *Image courtesy of SS Moyie National Historic Site*

**The advent of a railway link east to Quebec spurred the development of a francophone community in BC.**
*CPR Archives, BR213*

The CPR energized the province's economy, which was based in natural resources consistent with the National Policy. Furs, coal and gold were already exploited; now wood, fish and other minerals joined the mix.

Rail construction spurred demand for lumber, and the line's completion opened up new markets and sources of supply. Just east of British Columbia lay the future provinces of Alberta and Saskatchewan. Their largely unforested terrain made them suitable markets, and lumber sales doubled in the decade following 1886. As settlement grew on the prairies, BC mills pioneered new products, including prefabricated houses. Lumber also went to Asia, South America and Europe.

Fishing became profitable when a new industrial process for rolling out thin sheets of metal made it possible to preserve the abundant resource of salmon in tin cans. Alexander Ewen, a Scots entrepreneur who had been sending salted salmon to England, first used the process in 1870. He exported three hundred cases, each containing a hundred squat cans holding a pound (just under half a kilogram) of salmon, from a cannery on the Fraser River. Seasonal canneries, mostly financed by capital from outside the province, soon dotted the British Columbian coast. The first one operated on the Skeena River in 1877, followed by others on the Nass River and at Rivers Inlet. British Columbian canned salmon became a staple in many British households.

Above: **Before the days of power saws, cutting down BC's big trees was gruelling labour. Handfallers used temporary steps called springboards to get up where the chopping was easier.**
*Image B-06584 courtesy of Royal BC Museum, BC Archives*

Opposite: **As the lumber trade gathered momentum, skid roads and horse teams were needed to move logs from deeper in the forest.**
*Painting by Bus Griffiths, courtesy of Courtenay Museum and Archives*

**The Art of Logging**

British Columbia's large trees—cedar often towering 50 metres (over 150 feet) high and 5 metres (18 feet) in diameter, and Douglas fir at over 60 metres (about 200 feet) the tallest tree in Canada—made logging a challenging task. Novelist Bertrand Sinclair wrote in *The Inverted Pyramid*, "The Pacific Coast logger . . . is master of an intricate technique as applied to the handling of enormous timbers by powerful and complicated machinery. The BC woods is no place for the sluggish of brain or hand." Loggers felled the giant trees by climbing up on springboards jammed into notches a metre or more above ground, where the tree was thinner and the cutting easier.

Teams of horses or oxen dragged cut logs along a greased skid road resembling a railway without rails to the nearest body of water. In the early twentieth century animal teams gave way to donkey engines. These steam-powered engines mounted on sleds used long cables winched in on drums to yard logs out of the woods either onto railcars or into the water.

The huge tree stumps left behind so many years ago still dot many parks, including Pacific Spirit Park adjacent to the University of British Columbia.

**Fishing for a Living**

"Fishing is quite complicated and that's what is interesting," said one early practitioner. "You have to find where to go and when to put in your net, you have to think how best to use it each time and place, for high tide and low tide, when the wind is blowing and when it's calm."

Most early boats were small, hand-powered gillnetters. Their nets' mesh was big enough to allow free passage of undersize fish but small enough to capture salmon of the desired size. A fisherman's daughter explained, "The net is rigged with surface floats and sinkers and hangs like a curtain in the water. The salmon swim into the mesh and are caught behind the gills, hence the name gillnets."

Purse seiners were an advance on gillnetters. Fishers in large power boats set bigger nets around schools of fish, then closed a purse-line on the bottom rather like the tie on a pouch, sometimes trapping tonnes of fish. Net-caught fish were canned. Trollers used a hook-and-line technique to catch higher-quality salmon intended for sale fresh or cured.

**A commercial salmon fishing vessel trolls its lines off BC's Central Coast.**
*Photo Chris Harris*

Colourful labels helped to market BC's canned salmon in England. *Image I-61591 courtesy of Royal BC Museum, BC Archives*

**The Unique World of Salmon Canning**

Salmon canneries were large factories employing hundreds of people, often located far from the nearest settlement, and operating only a few months a year. At the peak, there were over a hundred working in remote bays and inlets along the BC coast. One typical operation was described thus by a young employee: "The cannery employed about 300 men and women, 150 inside and the remainder fishing. Chinese, hired on contract through a boss-Chinese, were the backbone of the canning operation. They cut and slit fish, fired the retorts and during the winter, even made cans. Tsimshian, Salish, Kwakiutl and other Indian women filled tins, and a handful of whites supervised, kept books and managed the plant."

For all of the hard work and racial separation, salmon canning gave opportunities for sociability that would otherwise not have been possible. Friendships were forged, husbands and wives found, and money got to last the coming year. The canneries provided seasonal employment to women, particularly aboriginal, offering opportunities not found in other industries. In the twenty-first century, many former cannery workers still look back fondly on the experience.

Skilled Chinese and aboriginal labourers were crucial to the cannery industry. *Image D-08373 courtesy of Royal BC Museum, BC Archives*

**The Kootenays at Work and Play**
Mattie Gunterman brought her plate camera to the West Kootenay in 1898. The result is a remarkable testimony to everyday lives, which for men revolved around a mining boom-and-bust, and for women around whatever jobs they could get.

*Illustration by Shelley Fearnley*

In the 1890s hardrock mining and entrepreneurship expanded north from the United States into the Kootenays. High-grade deposits of silver, copper, lead and other metals came into production, and the communities of Nelson, Rossland and Trail sprang into being. In a pattern repeated many times in the province's history, speculation was rife. From settlers and prospectors to international investors, people suddenly believed they could make their fortune overnight. Almost one in five British Columbians lived in the East and West Kootenays in 1901, by far the largest proportion the two regions would ever contain.

A scarcity of arable land meant that farming never took hold in British Columbia as it did elsewhere in Canada, where at least half of all employed males worked in agriculture. In British Columbia the proportion was under one in five. Farming was most profitable on southeastern Vancouver Island, on some Gulf Islands and in the Fraser Valley. Ranching flourished across the large interior plateau extending from the Cariboo–Chilcotin through the Okanagan Valley.

The railway also furthered population growth by encouraging migration from within Canada. The number of British Columbians who had been born elsewhere in Canada mushroomed from 35,000 in 1881 to 120,000 by 1891. Others came from farther away. The province's remoteness encouraged dreamers seeking a new beginning in what they saw as the far edge of the world. Among them were Norwegian idealists who settled at Bella Coola on the Central Coast in 1894, Danes who made for Cape Scott on the northern tip of Vancouver Island in 1897 and Finnish utopians who headed to Sointula on nearby Malcolm Island in 1902.

**As with many BC towns, the mine came first and Rossland grew up around it, fuelled by the gold of the Monashee Mountains.** *Image B-04823 courtesy of Royal BC Museum, BC Archives*

**The Chilcotin plateau made excellent ranchland.** *Photo Vance Hanna*

**The Emergence of Chinatowns**

Chinatowns reflected both the racism of the social mainstream and our human tendency to socialize with others like ourselves. Chinese labourers brought to work on the CPR were left to shift for themselves wherever they happened to be working last. They set up in jobs that no one else wanted and became servants, laundrymen, labourers, market gardeners and owners of small stores and restaurants. Newer arrivals did much the same. A son recalled how his father borrowed the money in order to immigrate in 1906 and, on arriving, "washed strangers' shirts and ironed them for a dozen years in Vancouver's Chinatown" to pay off the loan. Some went to great lengths to secure a wife from home, but many passed their leisure in the dominantly male settings of Chinatowns. Emily Carr observed how in Victoria, "when work was done . . . off they went to Chinatown to be completely Chinese till the next morning."

**Painting by Emily Carr.** *Image PDP00595 courtesy of Royal BC Museum, BC Archives*

Top: **Wah Chong laundry, Vancouver. Once the railway was built, Chinese labourers survived by operating services such as laundries and restaurants.** *City of Vancouver Archives, SGN 435.1*

Many Chinese helping to construct the CPR put down roots where they were last employed, and others made their way to the Chinatowns that grew up in Victoria, Vancouver and other communities. British Columbians born in Asia approached 10,000 by 1891 and doubled by the end of the century. By then the total included small numbers from Japan and India. The province's population grew from 50,000 in 1881 to almost 180,000 by 1901.

**By 1901 there were 4,600 Japanese living in BC, 97 percent of all the Japanese in Canada.** *Image C-07918 courtesy of Royal BC Museum, BC Archives*

**Conservative lawyer Richard McBride introduced party politics to BC, became premier in 1903 and served for twelve years. Painting by Victor Albert Long.** *Image PDP02261 courtesy of Royal BC Museum, BC Archives*

British Columbian expansion redefined provincial politics. Despite the exclusion of all people of Chinese, Japanese and Indo-Canadian ancestry as well as aboriginals and women, the number of voters reached 47,000 in the 1900 election. The growing impersonality of provincial life made it less acceptable for BC to be governed by premiers whose prestige rested on personal influence and patronage. By the end of the century, ministries were falling to scandal so quickly they scared away potential investors.

Political parties based on agreed values and goals, as existed elsewhere in Canada, began to be discussed. One of the enthusiasts was Richard McBride, a lawyer born in New Westminster, who in 1903 became premier under the banner of the Conservative Party. When his opponents banded together as Liberals, political parties became a fact of life in British Columbia. Previous premiers had held office for about two years on average; McBride broke the pattern by remaining in charge for a dozen years.

Many British Columbians, including McBride and the Conservatives, considered that the province could not carry out the ordinary business of government under the terms of union with Canada. The province's size, difficult terrain and scattered population made for exceptionally high routine costs of administration. A lack of manufacturing and high tariffs, ensured by the National Policy, obliged British Columbians to buy goods from central Canada at protected prices. The province, on the other hand, had to sell its own chief products—lumber, minerals, canned salmon—in world markets in direct competition with all other nations.

**Premier McBride started construction of BC's own railway, a north–south line called the Pacific Great Eastern. Though it took decades to complete, the PGE was energetically marketed as a vacation route to the trout-filled lakes of the BC interior.**

*Images PDP03239 (left) and PDP03240 (right) courtesy of Royal BC Museum, BC Archives.*

McBride sought "better terms" with the federal government. The compromise that he secured gave a short-term annual subsidy in exchange for the provincial government raising taxes and reducing expenses in an attempt to balance the budget. McBride took credit for the improvement in the BC economy that followed, but this was deceptive, for across Canada economies were expanding. Growing world demand for British Columbian commodities obscured the fundamental issue of the province's status in Confederation, and BC entered another of its periodic booms.

Keen to open up more of the province to resource exploitation, McBride encouraged rail construction by financially supporting two new lines. The Canadian Northern, which originated as a privately financed railway intended to encourage settlers into the prairies, entered British Columbia from Alberta north of the CPR line and paralleled it westward to Vancouver. The Pacific Great Eastern was intended to run from North Vancouver to Prince George, but only small parts got built during McBride's premiership. As well, the federal government subsidized a second transcontinental line to open up the prairies and then British Columbia's Central Interior region to agricultural settlement. Prince Rupert got its beginnings as the western terminus of the new Grand Trunk Pacific line.

Left: **Irrigation introduced at the turn of the century transformed the dry Okanagan Valley into a major fruit-producing region.** *Greater Vernon Museum and Archives #9126*

Below: **Okanagan apples became known around the world.** *Courtesy Kelowna Public Archives*

External investment complemented rail construction. The capital that could be generated within British Columbia was extremely limited. Expansion came primarily through outside impetus, as had already occurred with salmon canning and hardrock mining. Ontarian entrepreneurs were active not only in promoting rail lines but also in coal mining and forestry. British pounds tended to be less obtrusive, many taking the form of portfolio investment in government-guaranteed bonds underwriting new physical infrastructure or public utilities. Britons and Canadians engaged in land speculation, often on parcels near proposed rail lines, soon divided into small plots and sold off. Irrigation transformed the Okanagan Valley from ranching to small-scale fruit growing.

American dollars headed in several directions. They expanded the copper industry in the Kootenays and Boundary regions and financed a large pulp and paper mill on the south coast at Powell River. American investment was responsible for the tremendous growth of forestry, partly because the allocation of timber leases on Crown land long remained unregulated. By 1910 about 80 percent of forest land owned by the Crown had been leased, mostly to large syndicates.

**Doukhobors, a pacifist Christian sect who migrated to Canada from Russia, formed communal settlements in the Kootenays.** *Image C-01356 courtesy of Royal BC Museum, BC Archives*

Population growth fuelled the economy. As part of the National Policy, the Canadian government launched an immigration campaign to attract agricultural settlers into the prairies to produce raw materials and purchase manufactured goods from central Canada. British Columbia also benefited from the federal initiative. Britons in particular found the province attractive, in part because of its earlier colonial status and perhaps because of its name. The number of British-born grew twenty times, from 6,000 in 1881 to 116,000 by 1911.

The province continued to appeal to idealists seeking escape from the larger world. Among their number were Doukhobors, members of a communal religious group with origins in Russia, who settled in the West Kootenay and Boundary regions from 1908 onwards. In the 1920s Mennonites began arriving from Russia, some via Germany, also as intact communities. Settling near Prince George, at Yarrow and Clearbrook in the Fraser Valley and at Black Creek on Vancouver Island, they shared with Doukhobors a commitment to self-sufficiency premised on religious beliefs.

Geographical proximity meant that British Columbia, alone among the Canadian provinces, continued to attract immigrants from Asia. Sikhs from India often arrived with lumbering experience and tended toward that occupation, just as Japanese were most likely to become fishermen or small-scale farmers. British Columbians born in Asia approached thirty thousand by World War I. In sharp contrast, aboriginal numbers fell to an all-time low of just over twenty thousand by 1911.

British Columbia's overall population more than doubled in the first decade of the twentieth century to almost four hundred thousand. It moved upward to half a million by the beginning of World War I, which effectively curtailed large-scale immigration into Canada until the 1960s.

The benefits of growth increasingly filtered through Vancouver, whose population surpassed a hundred thousand by 1911, over three times that of the provincial capital of Victoria. No other

BC city approached Vancouver in size and influence. Establishment of the University of British Columbia there in 1908 only confirmed its pre-eminence. Vancouver acted as a service centre to an expanding hinterland, one that eventually encompassed the entire province except for the Kootenays and the Northeast, which looked to the prairies. By 1911 almost half of British Columbians lived in the Lower Mainland region that extended from Vancouver through the Fraser Valley.

**Sikh immigrants often favoured the sawmill industry. Here a group of North Pacific Lumber Co. workers at Barnet on Burrard Inlet east of Vancouver pose for the camera.**

*Philip Timms photo, Vancouver Public Library, VPL 7641*

**Vancouver's Hastings Street in the early twentieth century. Vancouver operated electric streetcars until the 1950s.** *Painting by Brian Croft*

**Vancouver Spreads Its Wings**

In the years before World War I, Vancouver came into its own. Some office blocks were erected by speculators to rent to small companies, but numerous insurance and shipping companies, banks, hotels, wholesalers and retailers built their own quarters. Some 200 kilometres (120 miles) of electric street railway extended Vancouver's reach across the Lower Mainland.

Social amenities developed apace. English Bay, not far from the much-loved Stanley Park, prided itself on its pier, dance pavilion, bandstand and beach overseen by volunteer lifeguard Joe Fortes. The young Barbadian arrived as a deckhand in 1885, built a small shack on the beach across from the attractive eight-storey Sylvia Court apartment block constructed in 1912—today a hotel—and taught a generation of young Vancouverites to swim.

Wherever men and women resided across the sprawling province, the tremendous expansion of free-enterprise capitalism during the early twentieth century had an enormous impact on their lives. Resource exploitation—which threw men together in jobs that were often tedious, dirty and hard—combined with urbanization to make British Columbians more aware of the inequalities that marked many lives. The drive to improve working conditions and quality of life extended from the workplace into the home. Some workers sought change through the ballot box, but direct action exercised a greater appeal. During the early twentieth century more strikes broke out in British Columbia than in any other province.

Activism was not confined to men or to the workplace. The movement for social reform was a largely female, white, middle-class enterprise in which women's traditional role within the home extended outward to the community. The Protestant churches sanctioned this; increasingly they felt an obligation to improve this world as well as prepare their adherents for the next one. Two issues that especially agitated social reformers were temperance and female suffrage.

Even as social reform was gaining impetus, the early twentieth-century economic boom ran its course. By 1912 capital was pulling back in the realization that much of the dynamism was little more than boosterism. The political situation in Europe was deteriorating, culminating in Britain's declaration of war against Germany in August 1914.

World War I affected everyone. Patriotism became the order of the day. British Columbia had the highest per capita volunteer rate in Canada at just over ninety per thousand population. The province's still uneven sex ratio played a role, as did its British ethos.

In reality British Columbians of every background volunteered for service, including members of the aboriginal, Chinese, Japanese and Sikh communities. Victory in 1918 came at a cost: 6,225 of the 55,570 British Columbians who served in the war died and another 13,000 were wounded. The influenza epidemic that broke out across much of the Western world in 1918 was a cruel aftershock that claimed another 4,000 or more BC lives.

During the war, McBride's premiership finally came to an end. His resignation in 1915 benefited social reformers as well as the political opposition. The Liberals made prohibition and suffrage part of their winning 1916 election campaign; the ballot included successful referendums on both, and legislation soon followed.

Above: **The 102nd Battalion (North British Columbians) marches down the main street of Comox on its way to war, June 1916.** *Photo courtesy of Comox Archives and Museum*

Top left: **War bond campaigns occupied the home front on Canada's entry into World War I.** *Image PDP03537 courtesy of Royal BC Museum, BC Archives*

Left: **Vancouver women organized volunteer groups to support BC troops going off to the Great War.** *Stuart Thompson photo, City of Vancouver Archives, MIL P36*

**Anti-Asian discrimination reached a low point with the harsh treatment of Indian immigrants aboard the ship *Komagata Maru*, which languished in Vancouver harbour for two months in the summer of 1914 before being driven off by a gunboat.** *Leonard Frank photo, Vancouver Public Library, VPL 6232*

**Women and the Right to Vote**

At the time British Columbia became a province, very few considered that women should have the right to vote. A woman's place was in the home under the direction of first her father and then her husband. The relationship between the sexes was summed up in Emily Carr's description of her parents. "Mother was Father's reflection . . . No one dreamt of crossing his will. Mother loved him and obeyed because it was her loyal pleasure to do so." By the early twentieth century, attitudes were changing. The opposition Liberals made women's suffrage part of their successful 1916 election campaign and BC women finally received the right to vote and run for office in provincial elections on April 5, 1917, a year before Ottawa extended the same rights to federal elections. The first female MLA was Mary Ellen Smith, who in 1918 won a Vancouver by-election to succeed her late husband.

The limits to reform became apparent at war's end. A general strike in Winnipeg in the spring of 1919 made clear that the government could only be pushed so far. Trade unions continued to exist across British Columbia, but the movement as a whole stalled. Partly because men still outnumbered women, prohibition similarly floundered. A repeal plebiscite was passed in 1920, making BC the first English-Canadian province to again permit the sale of alcohol, if under controlled conditions.

On the other hand the Liberal government caught the reform mood. The provincial legislature enacted a spate of legislation that created a civil service, initiated workers' compensation, provided for neglected children, gave pensions to needy mothers, established public libraries and expanded public schooling.

At the same time, civil rights reform for minorities was still years away. Immigration from Asia was increasingly restricted in various ways and the right to vote was denied.

Despite the prevalence of discrimination, which reflected attitudes across North America and beyond, racial minorities stood their ground. Many held jobs that others might see as menial, but they provided a living. Indigenous peoples drew on traditional ways and adapted to any new possibilities that came their way. British Columbians of Asian descent tended to cluster together to escape discrimination but also to support each other. Many blacks who had arrived during the gold rush had returned home following the American Civil War. Those who remained lived with dignity, as did indigenous Hawaiians who had arrived with the fur trade and mainly settled on coastal islands.

By the early 1920s key aspects of today's British Columbia were in place. Provincial governance was overseen by political parties that acquired their authority through periodic elections. Outside capital had developed an economy based in primary resources. Dependence on world markets for the sale of products made boom-and-bust cycles inevitable. British Columbia's distinctive economy, together with its faraway location, created tensions with the federal government.

Left: **Mary Ellen Smith, the first female MLA.**

*Image B-01563 courtesy of Royal BC Museum, BC Archives*

Cecelia Naukana, her husband George Napoleon Parker and their five children. From the early 1800s onwards, many Hawaiians like Cecelia's father William Naukana came to the Pacific Northwest to work in the fur trade and intermarried with First Nations families. *Photo courtesy of Salt Spring Island Archives, 2004004007*

## Vancouver's Booming Waterfront

The Vancouver waterfront was the city's heartbeat. From there canned salmon was shipped to England and lumber was exported around the world. Raw silk, which had a short shelf life, arrived by Empress liner from China to speed by train across Canada and then to the United States or England before it spoiled. Thirty or forty vessels might need to be unloaded and loaded in a matter of days, and speed was of the essence. First Nations men living on Burrard Inlet's north shore became renowned for their longshoring skills. Ed Nahanee, a career longshoreman of Squamish and Hawaiian heritage, described the satisfaction that came from a job well done. "When you went home, you went home feeling good, and the next morning you got started and you were all there again and away you go again. That was the spirit in those days. If I had to live my life over again, I'd do the same thing. I don't care how dirty it was. We were a part of each other."

NUMBER 85605

DOMINION OF CANADA

NEW C.I. 5 SERIES

IMMIGRATION BRANCH – DEPARTMENT OF THE INTERIOR

RECEIVED FROM

Lee Don whose photograph is attached hereto, on the date and at the place hereunder mentioned, the sum of Five Hundred Dollars being the head tax due under the provisions of the Chinese Immigration Act. The above mentioned party who claims to be a native of Lai Kok in the District of Hoy Ping of the age of 22 years arrived or landed at Victoria, B.C. on the 23rd day of July 1918 ex Kashima Maru The declaration in this case is C.I.? No 31926

Dated at Vancouver on 2nd August 1918

A. L. Jolliffe

CONTROLLER OF CHINESE IMMIGRATION.

In 1885 the government began imposing on Chinese immigrants a $50 head tax that had risen to $500 by 1903. In June 2006, Prime Minister Stephen Harper formally apologized and announced redress payments. *Vancouver Public Library, Special Collections, VPL 30625*

The making of British Columbia did not equate with its becoming a single, unified province. Distances were too great and the terrain too onerous. First Nations and people of Asian heritage were deprived of full citizenship. The promise that British Columbia gave had yet to be realized.

6260

# 4

# Growth of a Province

British Columbia did not come into its own overnight. A recession followed World War I, and afterward British Columbia once again boomed. International demand for lumber and minerals set the pace. The Panama Canal, which opened in 1914, made Vancouver an important transshipment point for prairie grain that had once travelled east by train. The adjacent municipalities of South Vancouver and Point Grey amalgamated with Vancouver in 1929, setting the city's present southern boundary at the Fraser River.

Previous pages: **BC industry boomed after World War I and again after World War II. Mural by Orville Fisher**. *Image PDP02285 courtesy of Royal BC Museum, BC Archives*

**Car Culture**

The automobile was a defining motif of the roaring '20s. In 1922 drivers began using the right side of the road, not in rejection of British practice but in the expectation that BC would link by road to the United States and neighbouring Alberta. Five years later a dirt road opened through the Fraser Canyon, the first non-rail link between the west coast and the interior since railway construction had destroyed parts of the Cariboo Wagon Road almost half a century earlier. It was also possible to drive south from Vancouver, Osoyoos or the West Kootenay and to link up with a paved road going east and west across Washington State. The province's natural north–south orientation reasserted itself. More and more British Columbians, even in outlying regions, became proud owners of Model T Fords. The total number of vehicles registered in the province rose from about 15,000 at the end of World War I to almost 100,000 by 1930.

In part for that reason Vancouver's population swelled to a quarter of a million by 1931. About 55 percent of British Columbians, out of a total now approaching 700,000, lived in the Lower Mainland, in a pattern that continues into the twenty-first century.

The good times encouraged new ways of living. Sparked by advertisements in Canadian magazines like *Maclean's* and *Chatelaine,* British Columbians increasingly bought what they needed or wanted, rather than making it at home. For families in remote areas, mail order catalogues from Eaton's, headquartered in Toronto, and Woodward's stores in Vancouver were a boon. For a northern Vancouver Island family, "The great thing about Woodward's was we could buy hay, oats, chicken feed, groceries and clothes all in the same order." Not only that, an early Woodward's catalogue claimed, "We carry a large stock of Umbrellas specially adapted for use in our British Columbia climate."

While many British Columbians got caught up in this new consumer culture, others found their pleasure in isolation from the larger world. What engaged them was their own piece of

Top left: **By 1930 there were almost 100,000 vehicles registered in the province of BC.** *W.J. Moore photo, City of Vancouver Archives, BU N274.2*

Above: **The Union Steamship Co. excursion ship SS *Lady Alexandra* at dock for a Union Grain Trade picnic in 1939. Grain became one of the port's main cargoes.** *Stuart Thomson photo, City of Vancouver Archives, CVA 99-2754*

land along a coastal inlet or in a far corner of the interior. The harsh reality that almost all the province is unsuitable for agriculture did not prevent a generation of believers from following their dreams. A pioneer Chilcotin rancher exalted, "We've found our country . . . a place that will be all our own . . . Our neighbours will be the wolves. Our music the call of the loon. Our beds will be the earth." Some of the most successful headed to the Peace River area beyond the Rocky Mountains, a fertile extension of the agricultural prairies.

Above: **Mail-order catalogues presented many new opportunities for rural buyers.** *Images courtesy Archives of Ontario, F229-5-0-96 and Hudson's Bay Company, Vancouver Museum, Add. MSS. 1085/608-C-7/file 6/Museum item # H976.16.22*

Left: **Spencer's department store, Vancouver. The 1920s were a boom time in BC and shopping was a new pastime.** *W.J. Moore photo, City of Vancouver Archives, CVA 1495-24*

The Great Depression humbled British Columbians. After the New York Stock Exchange crashed in October 1929, what first appeared to be another periodic recession turned into a full-blown disaster. The international markets that sustained the province's economy collapsed. Exports fell, jobs disappeared and the wages of those still fortunate to be employed were cut back. Common misery brought together people who might otherwise not have consorted with each other.

**The Great Depression Affected Everyone**

In *Waste Heritage,* Irene Baird's classic novel of the Great Depression in British Columbia, a father lamented, "I got three boys starin' ahead at nothing." Alternatives were sparse, one unemployed man recalled. "At this period and for many long years afterward, there was no unemployment insurance in Canada, no health or hospitalization insurance, nothing to ameliorate the stark fact of unemployment. It was private enterprise at its most brutal period."

Improvisation was the order of the day. Automobiles purchased so proudly just a few years earlier were turned into horse-drawn Bennett buggies—named after the prime minister—by being stripped down and fitted with wagon poles. Interior families made coffee out of roasted rye and soap from bear oil and moose fat. Visiting a farm family in the Peace River area, missionary Monica Storrs was "immensely impressed at the way the eldest daughter was making underclothes and even quite pretty cotton frocks out of old flour sacks!"

**Vancouver's Asahi baseball team provided a bright spot amid Depression gloom.** *Sanmiya Family Collection, Japanese Canadian National Museum 94/41.818*

Initially, provincial politicians seemed unable to grasp the seriousness of the situation. The Conservatives had returned to power in 1928 under Simon Fraser Tolmie, by family inheritance a throwback to the Hudson's Bay days. The party's commitment to applying business principles to government redounded to its disadvantage once the Depression hit. By 1931 unemployment across the province reached 28 percent, the highest in Canada.

The mainstream public was outraged. British Columbians had come to expect more from their provincial government than its traditional functions of maintaining law and order and encouraging private enterprise.

This growing sentiment in favour of a larger role for the state was reflected in the formation in 1932 of a new national political party, the Co-operative Commonwealth Federation. The CCF brought together reformist strands in Canadian society with the goal of forming a socialist government by democratic means. Many British Columbians embraced these ideas. While the opposition Liberals handily won the provincial election called in 1933, with 42 percent of the vote, the newly formed CCF captured 32 percent.

A strong leader strode onto the political stage in the tradition of James Douglas and Richard McBride. The new premier was Duff Pattullo, a Prince Rupert businessman and mayor who exuded self-confidence. Already identified with reform, the Liberal Party committed itself to dealing with social inequalities and unbridled capitalism. The CCF's shadow may have spurred legislation to reform taxation, restore social programs and initiate public works providing needed employment. Pattullo's background encouraged him to pay attention to the entire province in spurring economic development.

Depressed conditions persisted. The situation was intensified by unemployed men arriving from elsewhere in Canada; at least in BC they would not freeze to death, so they thought. Often "riding the rails," they tended to congregate in "jungles"—makeshift communities along the tracks—where they repeatedly protested their circumstances. They were joined by men fed up with the isolated work camps set up by the two levels of government. After the province restricted relief to all but provincial residents, about a thousand jobless men occupied the Vancouver post office, the art gallery and the Hotel Georgia in June 1938. Their violent removal by Vancouver police a month later became known as "Bloody Sunday."

**Small Pleasures of the Depression Years**

Sports gave one of the small pleasures of the Depression years. One of the top Vancouver draws was the Asahi baseball team based in "Little Tokyo" along Powell Street, whose generally small players gained renown for playing "smart ball." Lacrosse fans delighted in matches between New Westminster's Salmonbellies, named after a one-time seafood delicacy, and the North Shore Indians, whose name proclaimed their identity. Star player Simon Baker recalled that during the matches "we all talked Indian, and when we hollered in our language, the white man would look, and when he looked the other way, we were gone."

Opposite top: **Vancouver's Rev. Andrew Roddan, seen here distributing food at the city dump. He was a vociferous advocate for victims of the Depression.** *W.J. Moore photo, City of Vancouver Archives, Re N8.2*

Opposite bottom: **Without money to buy gas, Depression victims used horses to pull their cars, sarcastically dubbed "Bennett buggies" in honour of 1930s Prime Minister R.B. Bennett.** *Library and Archives Canada, accession no. 1976-138 NPC, C-087860*

Above: **During World War II, Victory Stamp campaigns sought to raise war funding among the public.**
*19750317-208, 19790385-085*
*© Canadian War Museum*

Below: **Trainees in the Canadian Women's Army Corps learn to stand at ease. They were among 90,976 British Columbians who served in World War II. Painting by Molly Bobak.**
*19710261-1554 Beaverbrook collection of War Art. © Canadian War Museum*

**War on the Home Front**

World War II affected all British Columbians, not just those who joined the military or were interned. Victory gardens, war saving stamps, rationing cards, nighttime blackouts and soldiers' parcels marked everyday lives. Industries traditionally closed to women, from plywood plants to pulp and paper mills, welcomed their labour. Children's school lessons now included the proper use of gas masks in case of an attack from the Pacific.

Pattullo increasingly came to believe that the province could only do so much. Like his predecessor Richard McBride, he spoke out for "better terms" in Confederation. Pattullo informed a federal commission examining inequities that 80 percent of manufactured goods coming into BC arrived from central Canada, whereas "75 percent of our main primary products, apart from agriculture, is sold in open competition in the world markets." By the time the Rowell-Sirois Commission concluded in 1940 that disparities did indeed exist and recommended the federal government exercise greater authority in relationship to the provinces, World War II had put the debate on hold.

Like the Great Depression, Canada's declaration of war against Germany in September 1939 affected everyone. As in World War I, the province had the highest proportion of men, and now also some women, serving their country. By war's end, 90,976 British Columbians of every background had served. Others volunteered for the Pacific Coast Militia Rangers, organized for civilian defence.

Above: **Japanese Canadian evacuees bid goodbye to friends. Following the 1941 Japanese attack on Pearl Harbor, 22,000 ethnic Japanese were evacuated from the BC coast in the name of military security.** *Library and Archives Canada, accession no. 1972-051 NPC, C-057250*

Left: **"Rosie the Riveter" breaks for coffee, Burrard Drydock, May 1943. Some thirty thousand workers, many of them women, took part in the wartime shipbuilding program at Vancouver, Victoria and Prince Rupert.** *Joseph Gibson, Library and Archives Canada, accession no. 1971-271 NPC, WRM 5204*

The war was particularly harsh to British Columbians of Japanese descent. After Japan's bombing of the American naval base of Pearl Harbor in the Hawaiian Islands in December 1941 and Canada's almost immediate declaration of war against Japan, everyone of Japanese background was evacuated from a 160-kilometre (100-mile) coastal strip. Thousands were dispatched to internment camps and their property was sold off.

Others reaped benefits from the war. Depressed conditions gave way to full employment. Manufacturing took off, owing particularly to ship and aircraft construction. In the wake of Pearl Harbor, Americans constructed a highway through the Northeast region of British Columbia to Alaska, where they feared an attack. Prince Rupert became an important supply centre for American military bases. By war's end in 1945, the north, at least in a psychological sense, had become part of British Columbia.

World War II became a turning point in attitudes toward British Columbians perceived as non-white. They themselves became less willing to accept their unequal treatment. While little opposition existed at the time to Japanese internment, in retrospect it was clear a great injustice was done to thousands of loyal Canadian citizens who posed no danger. Awareness grew among veterans of every background that some soldiers would return home to racism and discrimination. Change was also in the air more generally across North America.

While everyday discrimination took far longer to dissipate, legal restrictions came to an end. In 1947 the vote was given provincially to British Columbians of Chinese descent and to

**British Columbians in Service**

The first army unit in BC, the Victoria Pioneer Rifles, was formed in 1860 by forty-five American blacks. During World War I, British Columbians under Maj. Gen. Arthur Currie, a Victoria teacher, distinguished themselves in the taking of Vimy Ridge, the first major Allied victory of the war. In World War II, six BC regiments fought as distinct units, taking part in the ill-fated Dieppe invasion, the Italian campaign, the Normandy landing and the liberation of the Netherlands, among other actions. In 1997 BC's reserve army was redesignated the 39th Canadian Brigade Group with fourteen units, which continued many of the historic regimental names such as Duke of Connaught's Own Rifles, Seaforth Highlanders, BC Dragoons, Royal Westminster, Canadian Scottish and Rocky Mountain Rangers. Esquimalt remains the Maritime Pacific Headquarters of the Canadian Navy with two reserve units, HMCS *Malahat* (Esquimalt) and HMCS *Discovery* (Vancouver), and a sea cadet summer-training centre at HMCS *Quadra* (Comox). The Air Force maintains a base with about a thousand regular force, 19 Wing Comox, on Vancouver Island.

**Above: World War II fighter pilots Duke Warren and Stocky Edwards.**
*Photo Boomer Jerritt*

persons with origins in India, increasingly termed South Asians. Two years later the franchise was extended to Indians as well as the Japanese, who were only then permitted to return to the west coast. Segregated schools for Indian children gave way to their attendance at schools alongside other British Columbians. The longtime ban on the potlatch was removed.

Another boom followed World War II. Most everyone benefited from a long period of economic stability that extended, with a brief recessionary break from 1958 to 1962, into the early 1970s. The need to rebuild a heavily bombed Europe combined with industrial expansion around the world to increase demand for British Columbian products.

At the end of the war, much of BC was still isolated from the two major centres of Vancouver and Victoria. A soldier returning home to the Central Interior from fighting the war was appalled. "The roads in our area were impassable in the spring and fall; there was no electric power and little running water. I just couldn't believe what I'd come back to . . . no one seemed to give a damn." Men and women were in effect penalized for daring to reside outside of the province's southwestern tip.

The creation of British Columbia as a cohesive unit took precedence during the postwar years. A Liberal–Conservative coalition formed at the beginning of the war continued to govern through mid-century. Confirmed in power in a 1949 election, it gave priority to road construction and rural electrification. Prince George was linked by road to Dawson Creek, the Alaska Highway's British Columbian terminus. The privately run BC Electric Railway Company had favoured urban areas where profits were easier to reap, so in 1947 the BC Power Commission was established as a public body to provide electricity to outlying areas.

Opposite top: **The end of World War II was something for everyone to celebrate.** *City of Vancouver Archives, CVA 1184-3045*

**In the 1950s, independent family-operated shops like these along Robson Street gave Vancouver a cozy, small-town atmosphere.** *Photo Fred Herzog, courtesy of Equinox Gallery*

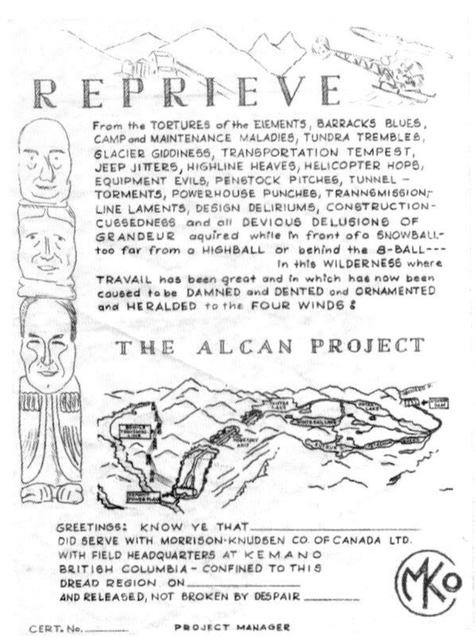

REPRIEVE

From the TORTURES of the ELEMENTS, BARRACKS BLUES, CAMP and MAINTENANCE MALADIES, TUNDRA TREMBLES, GLACIER GIDDINESS, TRANSPORTATION TEMPEST, JEEP JITTERS, HIGHLINE HEAVES, HELICOPTER HOPS, EQUIPMENT EVILS, PENSTOCK PITCHES, TUNNEL – TORMENTS, POWERHOUSE PUNCHES, TRANNSMISSION-LINE LAMENTS, DESIGN DELIRIUMS, CONSTRUCTION-CUSSEDNESS and all DEVIOUS DELUSIONS OF GRANDEUR aquired while in front of a SNOWBALL-too far from a HIGHBALL or behind the 8-BALL--- in this WILDERNESS where TRAVAIL has been great and in which has now been caused to be DAMNED and DENTED and ORNAMENTED and HERALDED to the FOUR WINDS &

THE ALCAN PROJECT

GREETINGS: KNOW YE THAT ______
DID SERVE WITH MORRISON-KNUDSEN CO. OF CANADA LTD.
WITH FIELD HEADQUARTERS AT KEMANO
BRITISH COLUMBIA – CONFINED TO THIS
DREAD REGION ON ______
AND RELEASED, NOT BROKEN BY DESPAIR ______

MKO

CERT. No. ______ PROJECT MANAGER

**A humorous certificate given to employees of the Alcan Project.**

*Courtesy of Kitimat Centennial Museum, Ernie Archer Collection, P00013*

Economic development followed suit. Forestry expanded into the interior, invigorating Prince George. Oil and natural gas exploitation began in the Northeast region, as was occurring on a larger scale in neighbouring Alberta. Asbestos mining began in the far Northwest. In 1951 the provincial government signed an agreement with the Aluminum Company of Canada (Alcan) to construct a large smelter southwest of Prince Rupert at what became the new town of Kitimat. The next year the long-dormant Pacific Great Eastern Railway reached Prince George.

A fundamental political shift transformed the province's capacity to take advantage of opportune economic conditions. Small-town merchant W.A.C. Bennett was among the many people who moved west because of the Great Depression; Bennett had departed the Maritimes for Alberta and finally BC's Okanagan Valley. He was part of a larger movement west. The number of British Columbians born on the prairies shot up from one in twelve in 1931 to over one in five by 1951. Some migrants supported the CCF, in power in Saskatchewan since 1944. Others adhered to the populist movement called Social Credit that ruled Alberta from 1935. Yet others such as Bennett joined the Socreds after breaking with established political parties.

By the time a provincial election was called in 1952, policy and personal differences had splintered the governing coalition and created widespread dissatisfaction with both of the old-line parties. The coalition tried to improve its chances by instituting a transferable ballot, which would permit voters to rank their choices.

The election held two surprises. The CCF received the plurality of votes, but after the transferable ballots were calculated Social Credit gained one more seat. Called upon to form a government, Bennett made clear his sensitivity to the province's diversity by including in his cabinet the first woman to hold a portfolio, a trade unionist, persons of non-British descent, hinterland British Columbians and former Albertans.

**Pack dogs and their owners on George Street, Prince George, 1953. Prince George attracted so many sawmills that it became known as the Spruce Capital of Canada.**

*W.D. West Collection, Fraser Fort George Regional Museum, P993.11.1.2252.2*

Left: **A line crew in Vernon, 1945. Following World War II, BC enjoyed a prolonged boom that put people back to work with a vengeance.**

*Photo courtesy of BC Hydro Power Pioneers*

Below: **In 1950 the Aluminum Company of Canada (Alcan) established a large smelter and hydro complex southwest of Prince Rupert, giving rise to the new city of Kitimat.**

*Photo Dwight Magee, Rio Tinto Alcan*

**Bennett Everywhere in Charge**

Part of the secret to W.A.C. Bennett's success as premier was his personality. Veteran journalist Bruce Hutchison wrote, "The fixed neon smile, the bustling salesman's assurance, the ceaseless torrent of speech, the undoubted talents of a small-town hardware merchant writ large and a certain naive, boyish charm are . . . the emblem and hallmark of a new province." Bennett was in charge everywhere. Hutchison became convinced that he was witnessing "a total revolution of the British Columbia spirit."

To resolve the stalemate with the CCF, Bennett called a new election just a year later and won a decisive victory. In the next election, after the province had returned to a traditional ballot, a Social Credit coalition was entrenched. The force of Bennett's personality continued to be decisive even after the CCF reorganized itself in 1961 as the more moderate New Democratic Party (NDP). Only in 1972, when Bennett had been in power for two decades, would the balance shift.

Building on economic initiatives already underway, the Socreds capitalized on the rising wages, prosperity and growing self-confidence across much of the Western world. Like his predecessors, Bennett tended to blame the federal government for his failures and took personal credit for any successes. He promised British Columbians what he liked to term "the good life," and for many years he succeeded.

Growth through rapid resource development became almost a secular faith within the Social Credit Party. The key to expansion lay in attracting large amounts of outside capital, and American dollars in particular arrived at unprecedented rates. By the mid-1950s over half the investment in a rapidly expanding forest industry came from the United States. Government policy favoured large corporations over the small "gyppo" operations of the past. As long-term

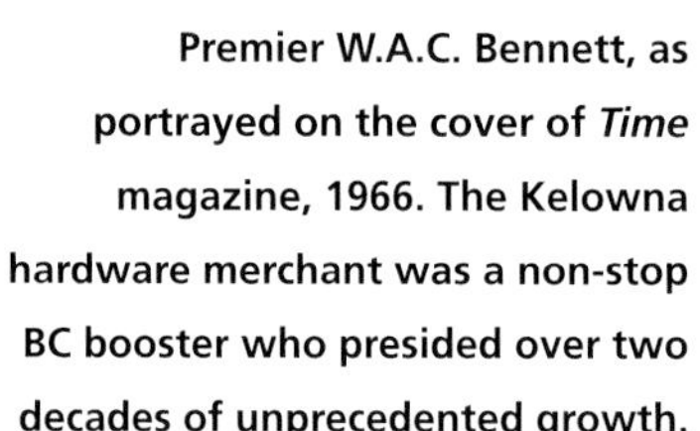

**Premier W.A.C. Bennett, as portrayed on the cover of *Time* magazine, 1966. The Kelowna hardware merchant was a non-stop BC booster who presided over two decades of unprecedented growth.**
*Painting by Henry Koerner, courtesy Kelowna Museums Society Collection*

leaseholders of Crown timber, the corporations were viewed as being more responsible stewards. Much of the expansion centred on pulp, and this too spurred the forest industry's consolidation into a handful of large, integrated multinational companies. The value of Canadian products exported from British Columbia grew fivefold over the two decades of 1952–72.

**The forest industry emerged as BC's leading economic generator in the post-war era, giving rise to large, integrated corporations like MacMillan Bloedel, Canfor, BC Forest Products and Doman Industries.**

*Photo Leigh Kirkwood*

**Forestry Giants**

While much of the revenue responsible for the growth of forestry originated outside of the province, the industry benefited enormously from entrepreneurs committed to British Columbia. Four giants stand out. A young Ontarian who came west in 1912 as the first chief forester, H.R. MacMillan went on to create one of the world's largest forestry companies, MacMillan Bloedel.

Otto, Leon and Walter Koerner, who left Czechoslovakia just before World War II, built Alaska Pine Co. Ltd. (later Rayonier Inc. and Western Forest Products) by finding markets for BC's vast stands of western hemlock, which were largely unharvested. Culturally sophisticated, they bequeathed much of their fortune to philanthropy.

After escaping from Austria on the eve of the war, Poldi Bentley turned his attention to the new technique of plywood. The company he and then his son Peter headed, Canadian Forest Products or Canfor, became the largest softwood producer in Canada. Their mills include a joint manufacturing venture with the Wet'suwet'en people at Moricetown in the Central Interior.

The son of Sikh immigrants, Herb Doman began selling wood and sawdust door-to-door from a second-hand truck on Vancouver Island. He eventually headed Doman Industries, a multi-faceted forestry company that at its peak spanned Vancouver Island and the adjacent mainland coast.

Above: **BC Ferries' newly-launched *City of Vancouver* (aka *Queen of Vancouver*) steaming out of Vancouver Harbour to take up her station on the Tsawwassen-Victoria run in 1962.** *Photo courtesy BC Ferries Archives*

Top: **The government-owned BC Ferry Authority was a key part of W.A.C. Bennett's strategy to stimulate growth by expanding infrastructure. These promotional decals were given free to customers.** *Photo courtesy BC Ferries Archives*

Right: **Airplane travel became an important mode of transportation, linking the BC interior and north to the rest of the province.** *Fraser Fort George Regional Museum, P982.48.73*

**Lessening British Columbia's Vast Distances Through Flight**

The airplane was fundamental to lessening distances across British Columbia and with the rest of Canada. Bush pilots exemplified a spirit of adventure. When a serious injury occurred in 1935 on a Chilcotin ranch, a seeming miracle ensued. The news got out over a makeshift telephone hookup, whereupon "a doctor flew in by float plane using huge bonfires as signalling beacons," being "the second plane ever to wing into the country." Two years later bush pilot Grant McConachie began the first scheduled—if irregular—service between such points as Prince George and Fort St. James. In 1939 Vancouver was linked to central Canada by Trans-Canada Airlines, which became Air Canada in 1965. Two years later the Canadian Pacific Railway purchased Grant McConachie's line to form Canadian Pacific Airlines, which would merge into Air Canada in 2000.

The 1950s brought a focus on creating infrastructure, which facilitated the big development projects of the following decade. During the first six years of Bennett's tenure, more money was spent building roads than in the entire history of the province. Air travel and water transport also expanded, including better ferry service linking the mainland, coastal islands and Vancouver Island. Travel across the vast province became convenient for the first time.

The W.A.C. Bennett Dam and generating station, Premier Bennett's crowning megaproject, was completed by BC Hydro in 1967. Located at the canyon of the Peace River near Hudson's Hope, it created BC's largest lake, Williston Lake. *Photo courtesy BC Hydro*

In the 1960s the emphasis shifted to megaprojects. The most significant depended on hydroelectric power. The Columbia River Treaty, signed in 1964 with the United States, initiated the construction of three storage dams in the Kootenays in exchange for a lump-sum payment by the United States for the downstream hydroelectric benefits that would result. The Peace River in the Northeast was harnessed by the mighty Bennett Dam, completed in 1967.

Social services expanded. Both the provincial and federal governments facilitated health insurance and special provisions for the young and the old in the form of family allowances and pensions. Educational opportunities grew at the post-secondary level. A college offering two-year programs was upgraded to the University of Victoria in 1963. A new British Columbia Institute of Technology opened in Burnaby just east of Vancouver the next year. Simon Fraser University began in Burnaby a year later. Community colleges offering both vocational training and two years of university transfer courses were established around the province, and some would eventually become four-year degree-granting institutions. More and more British Columbians had access to post-secondary education.

**Along with instant towns, BC got instant universities. Designed to order for the Bennett government by Arthur Erickson and Geoffrey Massey, Simon Fraser University opened atop Burnaby Mountain in 1965.**

*Photo courtesy Simon Fraser University*

**BC was an early hotbed of anti-war and environmental activism. Here demonstrators take to Vancouver streets in 1961 for a "Ban the Bomb" protest.** *Claude P. Dettlof photo, Vancouver Public Library, VPL 41905*

These shifts built on and reflected larger changes in attitudes. Deference to authority, long taken for granted, came under challenge. In the 1960s and '70s across the Western world, including British Columbia, restlessness gripped an entire generation of young men and women. They openly rebelled against their parents' emphasis on material possessions and conservative social conformity of all kinds.

Some adopted alternative lifestyles that were simpler and closer to nature. British Columbia offered prime opportunities to do so for young people from across North America. Going "back to the land," as it was sometimes termed, took many immigrants, largely American, to diverse locations ranging from the Kootenays to the Gulf Islands and adjacent coastlines. Often they formed collectives of like-minded individuals reminiscent of earlier idealists at Sointula and Bella Coola. Their common goal was self-sufficiency achieved by making their own garments, growing or catching food and constructing living quarters out of natural materials such as driftwood and logs. Others fought to reform the status quo toward greater equality in all aspects of life. Women resolved that their gender should no longer restrict their opportunities; persons long dismissed as inferior by virtue of their skin tones resolved that they should not be held back. In 1970, a group of idealists determined to combat environmental abuse and promote peace founded the committee that became Greenpeace, sowing the seeds of an international movement.

**Vancouver Greenpeace activists protest a visit by the US aircraft carrier *Ranger* in 1981. Later an international leader in environmental advocacy, Greenpeace was founded in Vancouver in 1970.** *Photo Brian Kent/*Vancouver Sun

Pride grew in being British Columbian. It became less necessary to move elsewhere, or be acclaimed elsewhere, to achieve recognition as an artist, writer or performer. Cultural venues multiplied, as did the number of homegrown publishers. Whatever the form of expression, agreement grew that a person's race or gender—and increasingly also sexual orientation and physical ability—should no longer determine access to British Columbia's opportunities.

The new medium of television and the national broadcaster, the CBC, encouraged a sense of distinctiveness. During the 1960s *Cariboo Country,* a dramatic series set in the Chilcotin, celebrated the ranching culture of the BC interior. Over the next two decades *The Beachcombers,* set on the Sechelt Peninsula, turned attention to a coastal fishing community, to the delight of audiences around the world.

The province's population continued to grow. A post-war baby boom occurred when British Columbians who had postponed their families decided the time was right. The good economic times encouraged Canadians to head west, not just from the prairies but from across the country. Immigration was a different matter. Canada accepted a few newcomers from Europe and elsewhere in the aftermath of World War II, but it was only in 1967 that federal policy once again encouraged immigration. Between 1941 and 1971, the number of British Columbians more than doubled to over two million and would almost double again by the end of the century.

**British Columbia's Own Western**

One of the first CBC dramas to be filmed on location, *Cariboo Country* was intended to counter the American westerns so popular on television. *Cariboo Country* depicted everyday life in the Southern Interior from the perspective of ranchers and First Nations people. All of the latter were portrayed by aboriginal actors, including Chief Dan George, who went on to Hollywood stardom.

**Above:** *Photo Franz Linder, CBC Still Photo Collection*

**The cast of *The Beachcombers* on location at Gibsons during its nineteen-year run as BC's most successful television series.**

*CBC Still Photo Collection*

**Nancy Greene.** *Photo courtesy of BC Sports Hall of Fame 6851.21*

## Olympic Triumphs

A string of Olympic triumphs sparked pride in British Columbians young and old. Many still recalled Vancouver sprinter Percy Williams's unprecedented gold medals in the 100 m and 200 m in 1928 and rejoiced as sprinter Harry Jerome took home a 100 m bronze in 1964. Four years later Nancy Greene won gold and silver in skiing, and Elaine Tanner won double silver in swimming. In 1972 Karen Magnussen gained a silver medal in figure skating. Among a string of Olympic triumphs, in 1984 Lori Fung won the first gold medal awarded at the Olympics in rhythmic gymnastics, and in 1998 Ross Rebagliati won the first gold in snowboarding.

## The Growth of Professional Sports

While professional sports operated in a limited way earlier, it was in the 1960s and '70s that they really came into their own in British Columbia. Since arriving in 1954, the BC Lions football club has won the Grey Cup five times, in 1964, 1985, 1994, 2000 and 2006. The Whitecaps soccer team, started in 1974, won the North American championship five years later. The Vancouver Canucks National Hockey League team has been a different story. Despite failing to win a Stanley Cup since their arrival in 1970, by 2008 they could boast the second-longest streak of sold-out games in the league, ahead of such pro sports meccas as New York and Toronto.

**Top: BC Lions quarterback Jerry Tagge (8) hands off to running back in a 1977 CFL game against the Hamilton Tiger Cats.** *Photo John Sokolowski*

**Above: The Vancouver Whitecaps won the North American Soccer League championship in 1979.** *Photo courtesy of BC Sports Hall of Fame 7324.1*

**Left: Prior to being a favourite NHL team, the Vancouver Canucks were the Pacific Coast League champions in 1945–46.** *Photo library Vancouver Canucks*

**Top left to right: Al Purdy** *(Photo D'arcy Glionna)*, **Sheila Watson** *(Photo Roland McMaster, Sheila Watson fonds, Special Collections and Rare Books, John M. Kelly Library, University of St. Michael's College)*

**Above left to right: Anne Cameron** *(Photo Peter A. Robson)*, **Peter Trower** *(Photo Barry Peterson and Blaise Enright-Peterson)*

### A Self-confident Literary Tradition

A self-confident literary tradition took hold in British Columbia. Some earlier writers, including Emily Carr and Ethel Wilson, evoked a strong sense of place, but now the number of writers grew. Some, like English-born Malcolm Lowry, Americans Jane Rule, Audrey Thomas and Paul St. Pierre, Maritimer bill bissett, Manitobans George Woodcock and Dorothy Livesay and Albertans Earle Birney and W.P. Kinsella, arrived from out of province. Among writers with their roots deep in British Columbia were Denise Chong from Prince George, Tom Wayman from Prince Rupert, George Bowering from the Okanagan, Patrick Lane from the Kootenays, Jack Hodgins from Vancouver Island's Comox Valley, Sheila Watson from New Westminster and Joy Kogawa and Wayson Choy from Vancouver.

Bill Bennett, W.A.C.'s son, showed some of his father's flair for megaprojects in building the SkyTrain, light rapid transit in the Lower Mainland, in 1986. *Photo Larry Scherban*

By the beginning of the 1970s, enthusiasm for W.A.C. Bennett's Social Credit was finally waning. The late sixties brought new, more complex attitudes to the fore and the aging premier's repertoire of construction projects and resource development had begun to seem passé. In 1972 the New Democratic Party (NDP), led by youthful Vancouver social worker David Barrett, stormed to victory with thirty-eight seats to the Social Credit's ten.

Barrett's NDP was an activist regime that enacted many reforms during its short time in office, including such lasting initiatives as public auto insurance (ICBC) and the Agricultural Land Reserve (ALR), which sought to halt development on farmland. In retrospect, Barrett and the NDP may have tried to do too much too fast, especially as the long post-war economic boom had finally ended in a global recession.

Meanwhile, the Social Credit Party was revitalized under a new leader, W.A.C. Bennett's son, William (Bill) Bennett. When Barrett decided to gamble on an early election call in 1975, two years before the end of his mandate, the NDP was swept from power. The economic downturn meant the younger Bennett headed a more austere administration than had his father.

After a three-year interlude under the New Democratic Party, Social Credit returned to power in 1975 under Bill Bennett. *Image I-68024 courtesy of Royal BC Museum, BC Archives*

The widespread opposition to proposed Socred cutbacks showed the changing nature of the province's workforce. Wage labourers in resource industries could be—and were—let go whenever the economy turned down. Four out of the five largest unions now represented public employees, teachers or other service and non-manual workers whose jobs were not market-dependent. When this group found itself targeted for wage freezes, rollbacks and layoffs, it resisted by banding together under an ad hoc front known as the Solidarity Coalition and was heading toward a general strike when dramatic last-minute negotiations between Bennett and union leader Jack Munro resulted in a compromise known as the Kelowna Accord.

Three of Bill Bennett's initiatives were reminiscent of earlier megaprojects. The Coquihalla Highway linked the Southern Interior to Hope in the eastern Fraser Valley, hence to the coast. ALRT was a high-speed transportation system crossing the Lower Mainland. Expo 86 was an international exhibition held in Vancouver in the summer of 1986 to encourage tourism.

**Expo 86**

Expo 86 raised British Columbia's profile on the world stage as never before. Featuring pavilions from sixty-four nations and numerous corporations, the international exhibition in Vancouver ran from May to October 1986. Many of its 22 million visits came from outside of the province and the nation, including 6.5 million Americans.

Tourism took off in the wake of Expo 86. Canada Place, built as the federal site of Expo 86, became a combined trade and convention centre, cruise-ship facility and hotel.

**Expo 86 catapulted BC onto the world stage, attracting over 22 million visitors.** *Photo Reimut Lieder*

Under Bill Bennett's successors Bill Vander Zalm and Rita Johnston, Social Credit held on to power as a shifting free-enterprise coalition, but by the end of the 1980s the party was discredited due to internal dissension and lack of vision. The New Democratic Party, led by Vancouver's former mayor Michael Harcourt, won the provincial election called in 1991, finishing the Social Credit Party as a political force in BC. Harcourt governed in a pragmatic, low-key manner that made headway in administrative areas like aboriginal land claims and land-use planning but encountered opposition on several political fronts, notably from environmentalists opposed to logging in Clayoquot Sound on Vancouver Island. Following Harcourt's resignation in 1996, former finance minister Glen Clark led the NDP to a second term. He did so despite losing the popular vote—39 to 43 percent—to a rejuvenated BC Liberal Party headed by another former Vancouver mayor, Gordon Campbell. Following Clark's resignation over allegations for which he would eventually be cleared, Dan Miller and Ujjal Dosanjh served briefly as premier, Dosanjh being the first South Asian premier in Canada. In the 2001 election, Gordon Campbell's BC Liberals engineered the greatest landslide in BC history, capturing all but two of the seventy-nine seats in the provincial legislature.

**A More Inclusive Political Mainstream**

BC's political mainstream broadened in the second half of the twentieth century. Elected an MLA in 1949, Frank Calder of the Nisga'a Nation was the first Indian to serve in a provincial legislature, just as Len Marchand, an Okanagan, became the first to be elected an MP in 1968. Marchand followed in the footsteps of Douglas Jung, who in 1957 was the first Canadian of Chinese heritage to sit in Parliament. In 1972 Rosemary Brown and Emery Barnes became British Columbia's first black MLAs, where they were joined in 1986 by Moe Sihota as the first South Asian to sit in a provincial legislature. Shortly after her election, Brown reminded her fellow MLAs how Mifflin Gibbs had been a black alderman in Victoria in 1866, over a century before. "We all are part of your history," she told them. In 1988, Hong Kong immigrant David Lam was named lieutenant governor, becoming the first Canadian of Chinese ancestry and only the second non-white to do so in Canada. In 2007 Stó:lo chief Steven Point became the first aboriginal person to be appointed lieutenant governor.

**In 1988, David Lam became the first Canadian of Chinese ancestry to be named lieutenant governor in Canada.** *Painting by Cyril Leeper. Image courtesy of the Office of the Lieutenant Governor of British Columbia*

Campbell used his overwhelming mandate to make the economy more competitive and market-based and to secure the 2010 Winter Olympics for British Columbia. In the next election, held in 2005, Campbell won a second majority, although the NDP recovered to thirty-three seats.

**Negotiating Modern-Day Treaties**

A century and a half after outsiders arrived in substantial numbers on the land we know as British Columbia, serious treaty making is under way. The Nisga'a Nation and the governments of BC and Canada signed the first modern-day treaty on April 13, 2000. As part of the settlement, nearly 2,000 square kilometres (770 square miles) of land in the Nass Valley was officially recognized as Nisga'a. Today the independent BC Treaty Commission oversees a made-in-BC process that brings First Nations and federal and provincial governments together around treaty tables.

Top left: **A procession of chiefs and dignitaries in New Aiyansh celebrates the final initialling of the historic Nisga'a Treaty in August 1998. A breakthrough for BC First Nations, the treaty was ratified by Parliament in 1999.** *Photo Ian Smith/*Vancouver Sun

**Canadian Firsts for British Columbian Women**

British Columbian women have scored important political firsts for Canadian women. In 1952, Tilly Rolston became the first female cabinet minister with a portfolio in Canada. In 1991, Rita Johnston became the first female premier in Canada. Two years later Kim Campbell became Canada's first female prime minister.

Left: **In 1991, Rita Johnson made history when she became Premier of BC, the first woman to hold the highest office in a Canadian province.** *Photo Denise Howard/*Vancouver Sun

Above: **Howe Sound Pulp and Paper Mill.** *Photo Dean van't Schip*

Right: **An ore truck at Huckleberry Mines Ltd., an open-pit copper mine near Tahtsa Lake in the Chilcotin.** *Photo Keith Douglas*

Opposite: **Big off-road logging trucks on Vancouver Island. The BC forest industry faced many challenges in the late twentieth century.** *Photo Chris Cheadle*

Although the turn of the century found the Lower Mainland continuing to lead in population growth and development, the rest of the province was not standing still. A new inland highway linked major points on Vancouver Island in the 1990s. The University of Northern British Columbia opened in Prince George in 1994. The university/college in Kamloops became Thompson Rivers University in 2005, the same year its Kelowna counterpart joined forces with the University of British Columbia. The vast distances separating British Columbians from each other continued to matter, but not quite as much as they once had.

The province's economy was more difficult to manage. The dependence on world demand for the products British Columbia had for sale ensured an uneven pattern of growth. The 1988 free trade agreement improved markets in the United States, but American lumber producers successfully lobbied for limitation on Canadian softwood lumber exports. A more serious challenge to the forest industry was the pesky mountain pine beetle, which threatened to wipe out 80 percent of the interior's valuable lodgepole pine. The province's location as Canada's gateway to the Pacific Rim paid dividends, as rapid growth in China and other Asian countries increased trade. Tourism, gaming, filmmaking and high-tech industries were major new revenue generators, while resurgent mining and petroleum industries led buoyant growth through the early 2000s.

**British Columbia's Homegrown Entrepreneurs**

British Columbia has been blessed with imaginative entrepreneurs. As well as revolutionizing grocery wholesaling, Tong Louie built up the IGA grocery store chain and the multi-purpose London Drugs. Lucille Johnstone grew RivTow, one of the largest towboat companies in the world. Wendy McDonald guided BC Bearing from a small machine shop to Canada's largest distributor of bearing and power transmission products. Milton Wong made his reputation as an investment manager. Frank Giustra has gone from investment banking to founding Lions Gate Entertainment to launching mining companies. Jimmy Pattison's multi-faceted business empire extends from sign companies to supermarkets to major forestry and fisheries holdings to the international Ripley's Believe It Or Not franchise.

The booms and busts marking the BC economy moderated to some extent, and expanding social services softened their impact on individuals and families. The nature of work was changing. Just one in five employed British Columbians were producing goods, compared to four out of five providing services. While Vancouver and the Lower Mainland continued to experience the most spectacular growth, the provincial capital of Victoria and the regional service centres of Kamloops, Kelowna, Nanaimo and Prince George also flourished.

One of the most important new influences on the economy and on British Columbian life more generally was the expanding environmental movement. Sensitivity grew globally and in BC on the need to maintain ecosystems, ensure biodiversity and practise sustainability.

British Columbia at the beginning of the new century was fundamentally different than in the 1920s, the Great Depression and World War II. It was in the war's aftermath that political will and new means of communication began to cut the vast distances that had divided the province. Difference no longer signalled separation and discrimination. BC had matured.

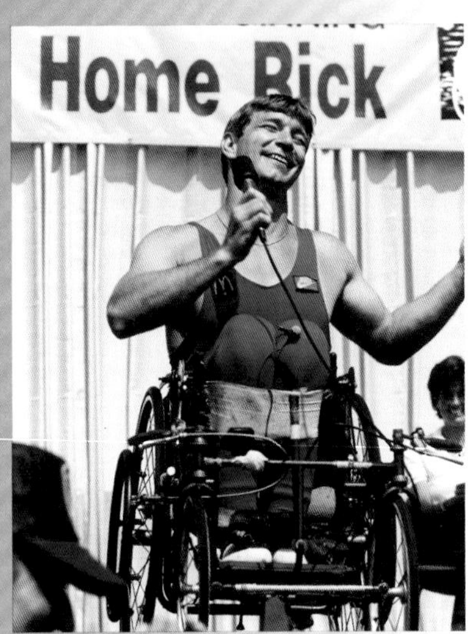


### The Legacies of Terry Fox and Rick Hansen

Nowhere is the spirit of British Columbia more evident than in the legacies of Terry Fox and Rick Hansen. Having lost a leg to cancer, in 1980 Terry Fox decided to run across Canada to raise money for cancer research. Rick Hansen, disabled in an auto accident, circled the world by wheelchair in 1985–87 to raise funds for spinal cord research. Both men gained worldwide attention and inspired millions.

**Above**: *Photos courtesy of BC Sports Hall of Fame and Museum 7551.8 and 7553.3*

### A Diversity of Creative Endeavour

Creative endeavour includes all disciplines. Identifying with the province are such diverse international successes as rock star Bryan Adams, classical pianist Jon Kimura Parker, visual artists Susan Point and Paul Wong, pop singers Sarah McLachlan and Nelly Furtado, *Generation X* novelist Douglas Coupland, photographer Jeff Wall, jazz sensation Diana Krall and crooner Michael Bublé. On winning multiple Junos in 2006, Bublé reflected how "I believe that had I started anywhere else but Vancouver, I would not be here."

Above: **(left to right) BC entertainers Michael Bublé, Nelly Furtado and Diana Krall.**

*Photos Ralph Orlowski/Getty Images, Juergen Schwarz/Reuters, T. Grant/Getty Images*

Top: **Two BC superstars, Sarah McLachlan and Bryan Adams, perform at a benefit concert in Vancouver in 2002.** *Photo Lyle Stafford/Reuters*

**Outstanding British Columbian Athletes**

Some of British Columbia's most talented athletes perforce live and work elsewhere. Maple Ridge's Larry Walker is renowned for his batting prowess, being named most valuable player in the National Baseball League in 1997. Delta's Jeff Francis has made his mark as a pitcher with the Colorado Rockies. Victoria's Steve Nash was named the National Basketball Association's most valuable player for two years running in 2005 and 2006. Among the numerous professional hockey players with British Columbian roots are Burnaby's Joe Sakic and Vancouverite Paul Kariya. Sakic was named the National Hockey League's most valuable player in 2001, and in 2002 he led the Canadian men's hockey team to a gold medal in the Olympics, where he was also named most valuable player. NHL star Kariya, the son of a Japanese internee, led the Canadian team to a silver medal in the 1994 Olympics and then played alongside Sakic in 2002.

**BC stars of pro sport: above, Larry Walker** *(R.C. Lewis/Getty Images)*; **top, women's soccer standout Christine Sinclair** *(Frederic J. Brown/AFP/Getty Images)*; **left, Steve Nash** *(Barry Gossage/NBAE/Getty Images)*

# 5

# The Promise of the Twenty-first Century

Understanding the past prepares us for the future. From whatever perspective we interpret them, the changes that have taken place in British Columbia over the past 150 years are breathtaking. Looking forward, there is every reason to think the future will be just as exciting.

British Columbia has been the only province to grow faster than the country as a whole in every Canadian census since joining Confederation in 1871. In 1901 British Columbia contained just 3 percent of the Canadian population, but that figure rose to 13 percent by the early 2000s; 175,000 people have become four million. Over the past century, BC's population has grown four times faster than Canada overall.

Previous pages: **Vancouver has a deserved reputation as one of the world's most beautiful cities.** *Photo Janis Kraulis*

This growth will continue. Demographers predict that by 2016, British Columbia's population will climb to five million, comprising 15 percent of the Canadian total. The main reasons will continue to be immigration and migration. BC's natural birth rate lags behind the Canadian average, but when you have the best place in the world to live, there is no shortage of outsiders willing to make up the difference.

Immigration has been good to British Columbia. Many of the province's most outstanding citizens have come from away. Alongside leaders like Duff Pattullo and athletes like Nancy Greene were entrepreneurs like H.R. MacMillan and David Lam spurring on the economy at critical moments. After the Great Depression it was prairie migrants like Jimmy Pattison and W.A.C. Bennett who led the way. Young people like the novelist William Gibson, the entertainer Jim Byrnes and the future cabinet minister Corky Evans arriving with the generational revolution of the 1960s and '70s continue to contribute to British Columbian communities big and small. As racial prejudice has loosened its hold, Asians and others long perceived as outsiders have taken a leading role in all aspects of provincial life. Unlike the rest of Canada in which most citizens live in the province of their birth, the majority of British Columbians continue to be newcomers who, in adapting to a new place, refashion the status quo.

Up until the mid-twentieth century the bulk of the immigrants attracted to British Columbia came from Britain and other European countries, but from 1981 onwards, over 60 percent have arrived from Asia, as opposed to only 16 percent from Britain and Europe. By 2006, 920,000, or almost one in four, residents claimed Asian descent. In the Vancouver phone book, Lee replaced Smith as the most common surname and the city took on a multicultural flavour that would astonish anyone who had not visited since the insular 1950s. It is now a modern, cosmopolitan metropolis where cultures of the world blend in a richly textured mosaic.

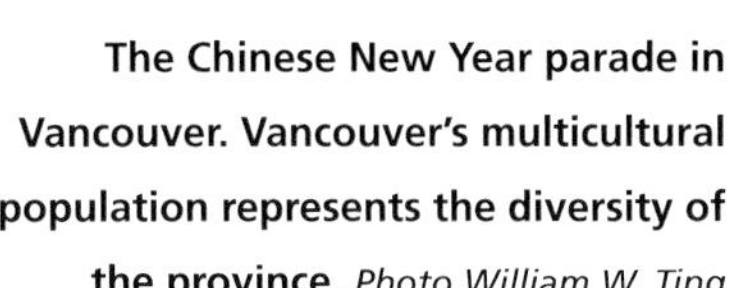

**The Chinese New Year parade in Vancouver. Vancouver's multicultural population represents the diversity of the province.** *Photo William W. Ting*

**The Pacific Gateway Swings Open**

Initially a liability, British Columbia's location on the far edge of the North American continent is now a boon. The colonists who took charge from 1858 onwards repeatedly protested the distance, real and psychological, that separated them from the centres of power in Canada and Europe. But the flip side of being farthest west is being nearest to the east, which gives the province a competitive advantage as the twenty-first century turns toward Asia.

**Above:** *Photo Ron Watts*

Top left: **The Gates of Harmonious Interest in Victoria's Chinatown.** *Photo Chris Cheadle*

Left: **World-class ski resorts like Whistler Blackcomb have made BC an international destination for winter recreation.** *Photo Randy Lincks*

Given British Columbia's appealing quality of life, immigration will continue to drive growth, although the origins of new arrivals may change, just as they have in the past. Hong Kong, once a major source of new arrivals, dropped off when political conditions stabilized there. The largest single source of new British Columbians has always been Canada itself, and that is unlikely to change.

Above: **Multiculturalism is deeply rooted in BC history. Steveston's first Buddhist shrine was built in 1928.**
*Photo Dannielle Hayes*

Top right: **A busker shows his stuff on Vancouver's Granville Island.**
*Photo Chris Cheadle*

Right: **Ukrainian dancers perform at Whistler Village.**
*Photo Bonny Makarewicz*

**Becoming British Columbian**

For most arrivals from within Canada, their province of origin appears to matter less than does their province of destination: a survey taken in 2005 found that three-quarters considered British Columbia their home as opposed to their province of birth.

**A Vancouver mother and daughter attend Vaisakhi, the important Sikh festival celebrating the harvest and the new solar year.** *Photo Tom Ryan*

**A Japanese Canadian woman poses in a traditional kimono before a mural celebrating BC's Japanese heritage at Chemainus, Vancouver Island.**

*Photo Boomer Jerritt*

**The impressively carved corner post in the Kitasoo Big House at Klemtu on the Central Coast.** *Photo Ian McAllister*

One sector of the British Columbian population that has not required outside assistance to keep its numbers up is the aboriginal community. For a century after contact with Europeans, First Nations numbers plummeted, dropping to nearly twenty thousand by the 1920s, causing speculation that indigenous peoples were on the road to extinction. Since that time the numbers have grown dramatically and may now stand higher than they were when Captain Cook visited Nootka Sound. Increasing one and a half times as fast as the general population, the First Nations presence in British Columbia can only be expected to gain strength as the years go by.

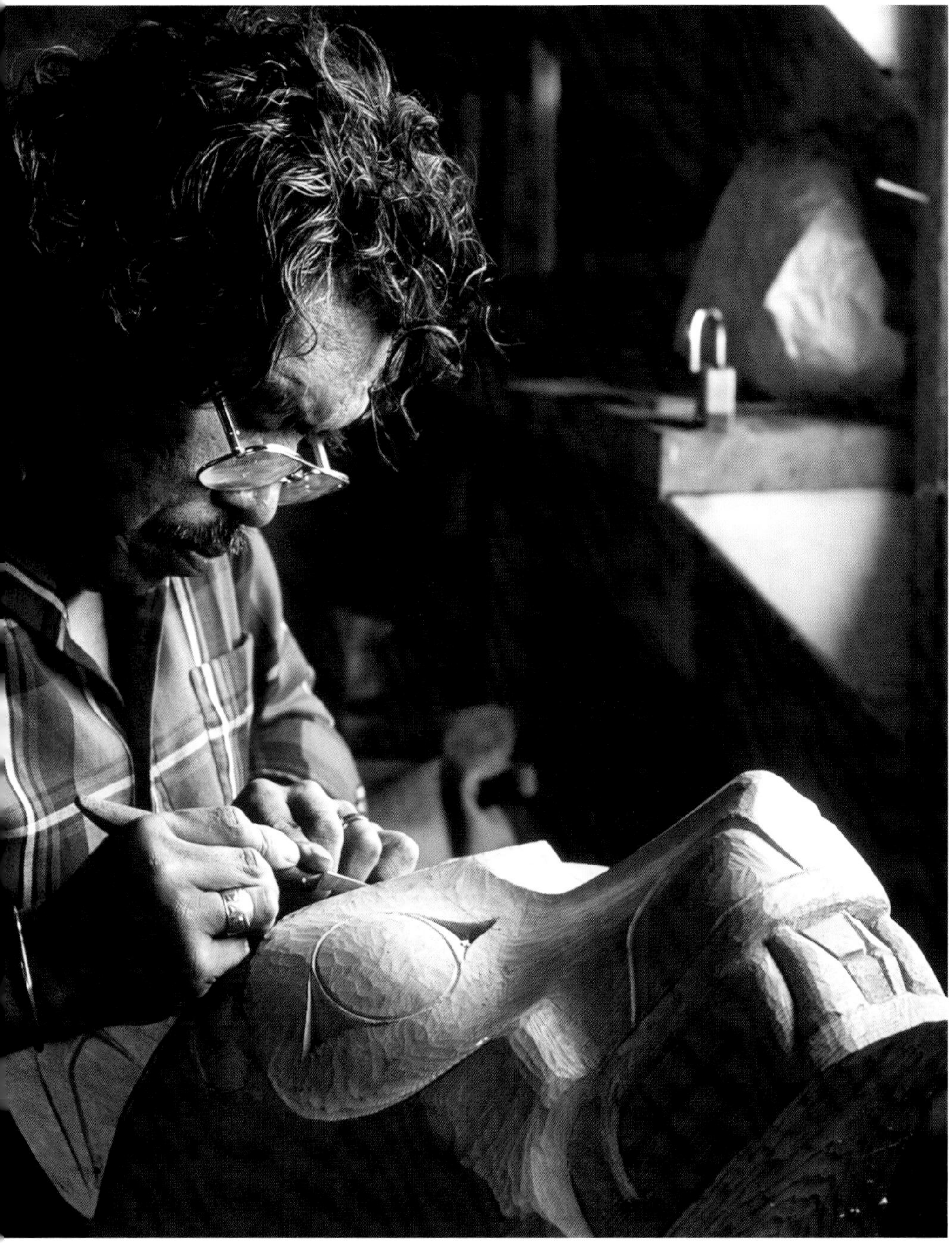

Above: **Lytton First Nation elders net a sockeye salmon from the Thompson River for their food fishery. Discussions on fishing rights are prominent in modern treaty negotiations.** *Photo Vance Hanna*

Left: **Nisga'a carver Alver Tait creates traditional sculptures in the Nass Valley.** *Photo Chris Cheadle*

Right: ***Continuing Cycle of Life*** **by Susan Point, a contemporary First Nations artist from the Musqueam Nation near Vancouver.**

*Photo courtesy of Coast Salish Arts*

Below: ***Raven and the First Men,*** **a monumental sculpture in wood by the late Haida master carver Bill Reid.**

*Photo Gary Fiegehen*

**The First Nations Cultural Renaissance**

When people in other countries think of British Columbia, many of the images that first come to mind—totem poles, cedar canoes, longhouses—are from First Nations culture. That is only likely to increase given the revival of traditional cultures during the latter half of the twentieth century. Ceremonials, fancy dancing at pow-wows, potlatching and the use of indigenous languages have all been invigorated. Instructed by such masters as Mungo Martin, Frieda Diesing and Bill Reid, an impressive generation of artists has come to the fore, including such modern masters as Daphne Odjig, Robert Davidson, Tim Paul, Susan Point, Dempsey Bob and Lawrence Yuxweluptun, to name a few. Their work gives BC an artistic style that is unique in the world.

Above: ***Legacy*** **by Andy Everson of Comox.** *Image courtesy of Andy Everson*

Left: ***Tapestry of Time*** **by Daphne Odjig of Penticton.** *Image courtesy of Hambleton Galleries*

**An Alkali Lake community leader mends a net as children watch with interest. The Alkali Lake band, west of Williams Lake, is a member of the Secwepemc Nation.**
*Photo Vance Hanna*

The long struggle by BC First Nations to achieve economic and social equality goes on, but recent progress in treaty negotiations constitutes an important step forward. Following creation of the BC Treaty Commission in 1993 and the signing of the landmark Nisga'a Treaty in 2000, negotiations were encouraged in late 2005 when Premier Gordon Campbell promised "a new relationship founded on reconciliation, recognition and respect of Aboriginal rights and title." In July 2007 the Tsawwassen First Nation south of Vancouver and five Nuu-chah-nulth First Nations on the west coast of Vancouver Island made treaties with the federal and provincial governments under the new treaty process. If momentum can be maintained, the day when all First Nations attain their rightful place in British Columbian society will have moved much closer.

The economy will continue to adapt to changing times, just as it has in the past. To the old way of thinking, the only "real" jobs are to be found in such traditional activities as logging, mining and fishing, which are decreasing as the various other factors intervene. British Columbia's labour force has undergone a revolution. Fifty years ago, the majority of the BC workforce was involved in the production of goods and only a minority in the production of services. Today that ratio is reversed.

This trend is solidly rooted in British Columbia being one of the most desirable places in the world to live. In an age when many people have the mobility to reside where they want, BC's superb quality of life has become one of its most valuable resources. People from all quarters and in all walks of life want the British Columbian experience. Some come as tourists, others as retirees, others still as workers with portable skills who put quality of life first when deciding where to live.

**A Retirement Haven**

British Columbia's natural beauty and moderate climate across parts of the province make it more than ever a haven for retirees from within Canada and without. Others seek rural locations in middle age, continuing to work through telecommuting. Some of BC's most popular retirement communities are located in the Vancouver Island region and include Qualicum Beach, Parksville, Sidney and the Southern Gulf Islands.

Above: **Lawn bowlers in Qualicum Beach, which has long been favoured as a retirement community.**

*Photo Boomer Jerritt*

Left: **Farmers' markets like this one at Kamloops satisfy the growing demand for local food.**

*Photo Chris Harris*

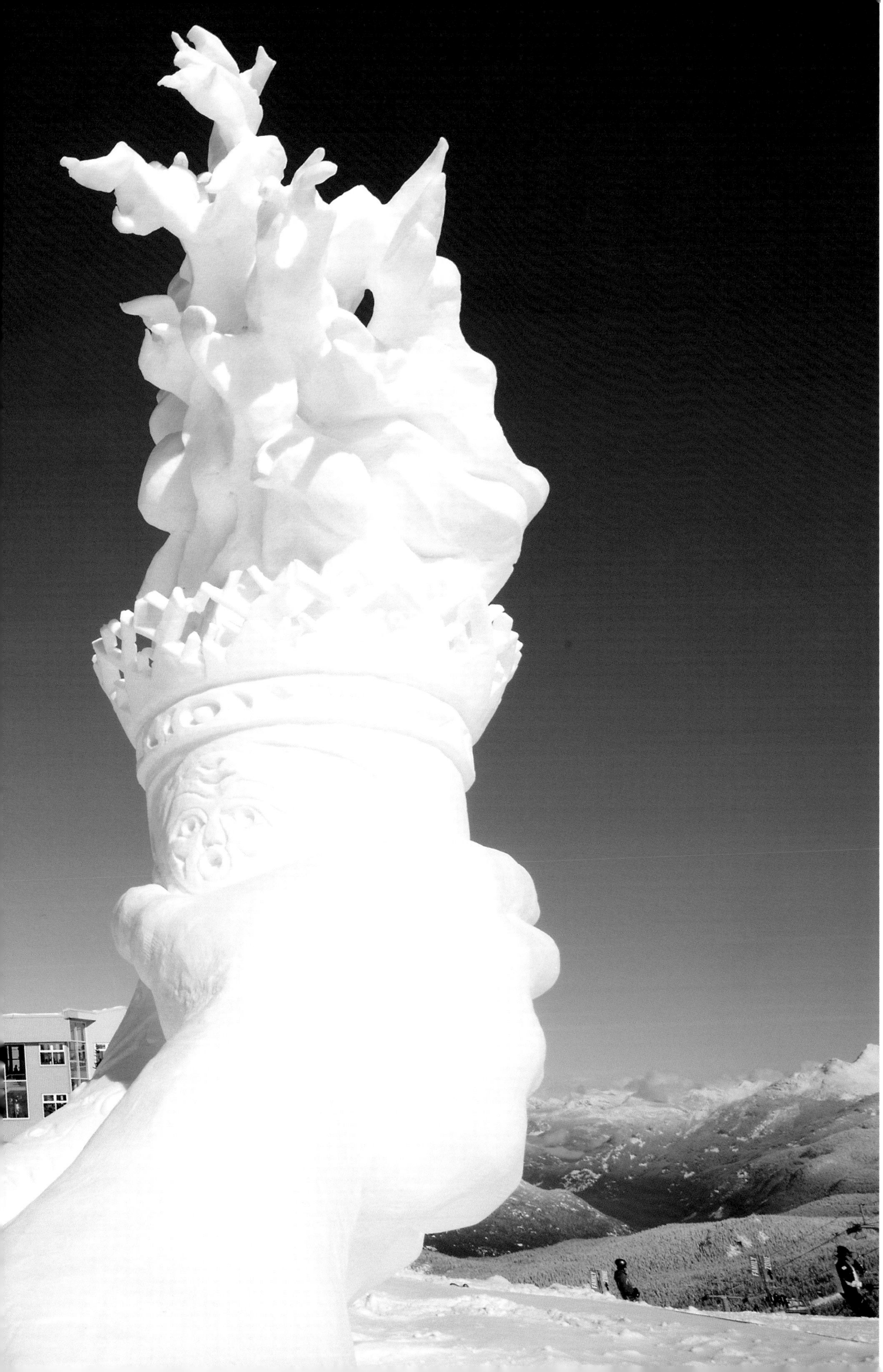

**The selection of Whistler Blackcomb and Vancouver as co-hosts of the 2010 Olympic and Paralympic Winter Games is emblematic of the energy and self-confidence with which the entire province meets the twenty-first century.** *Photo Toshi Kawano*

**A Tourist Destination**
The growing worldwide emphasis on nature and wilderness makes British Columbia's striking natural beauty and opportunities for outdoor recreation valuable commodities, attracting visitors from around the world. Over twenty million visitors arrive annually.

Above: **Pro surfer Ralph Bruhwiler makes a turn at a remote surf spot on the west coast of Vancouver Island.**
*Photo Jeremy Koreski*

Service industries like hospitality, entertainment, recreation, finance and food will all continue to grow in the twenty-first century, but they will not be the only show in town. A 2007 decision by the software giant Microsoft to open a large development centre in the Lower Mainland because of the area's "diverse population, its status as a global gateway" and the opportunity to "recruit and retain highly skilled people" is an indicator of the success with which BC has cultivated a favourable environment for information-age industries. The province abounds with technology companies, big and small, whose worldwide customer bases testify to their success. British Columbia is also home to the seventh-largest—and one of the fastest-growing—biotechnology clusters in North America.

Just because the new economy is thriving in British Columbia does not mean the old one is disappearing. Traditional resource-extraction industries continue to operate at high levels, especially mining and the Northeast petroleum and natural gas industry, which have become a leading engine of the British Columbia economy and will continue in that role for the foreseeable future. The still-impressive forest industry, though facing challenges on several fronts, is guaranteed to remain a major factor in BC's future simply because the province is sitting on one of the largest tracts of productive forest land left anywhere in the world. As long as trees continue to grow and wood continues to be one of humanity's favourite materials, BC will have the basic ingredients for a world-class industry.

The aspect of the future that occupies first place in the minds of British Columbians, according to a long series of opinion polls, is the environment. For whatever reason—perhaps because nature in BC is so spectacular and so central to residents' experience—British Columbians have long had a high level of concern about the state of the natural world. In 1970, the province was the birthplace of Greenpeace, the world's largest environmental organization, and it has been a centre of activism ever since.

**The *Coastal Renaissance*, the first of BC Ferries' three Super C-class vessels to begin service in 2008, pays a visit to Vancouver upon its arrival from the builders. The largest double-ended ferries ever built, the Super-C's carry 1,650 passengers and 370 vehicles.**
*Photo Glenn Baglo/Vancouver Sun*

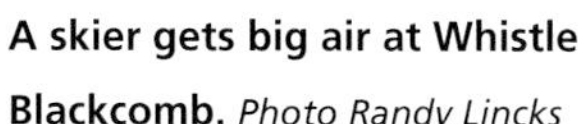
**A skier gets big air at Whistler Blackcomb.** *Photo Randy Lincks*

**Whistler Blackcomb**

Whistler Mountain, located 125 kilometres (75 miles) north of Vancouver, began to be developed during the mid-1960s. Within two decades, it and nearby Blackcomb Mountain had become British Columbia's premier ski resort, boasting the biggest vertical drops in North America and an especially long season running from November into June. Whistler Blackcomb did not take long to be discovered internationally, being repeatedly ranked at or near the top in competitive listings. The selection of Whistler Blackcomb along with Vancouver to host the 2010 Winter Olympics acknowledges the resort's supremacy. Whistler Blackcomb is complemented by a number of smaller ski resorts located around British Columbia.

**Wolves in coastal BC have adapted to foraging on the seashore and catching spawning salmon.**
*Photo Ian McAllister*

Environmental activism continues on many fronts. In recent years the BC government has created some of the largest protected wilderness areas in the world. Among them are the pristine Tatshenshini-Alsek watershed in the far Northwest characterized by glacier-cloaked peaks, wild rivers and lush valleys, home to grizzly bears and unusual plant communities; the Serengeti-like Muskwa-Kechika Management Area in the Northern Rockies; and, most recently, the 6-million-hectare (23,000-square-mile) Central Coast and North Coast Management Area. British Columbia has now protected 14 percent of its land mass, an area larger than Switzerland, Denmark and the Netherlands combined. In its 2007 Throne Speech,

A grizzly sow leads her cubs on a quest for food in the Bella Coola Valley. *Photo Michael Wigle*

the British Columbia government took the most aggressive stance of any Canadian government in combating global warming, calling for a 33 percent cut in greenhouse gas emissions from current levels by 2020. "This isn't going to happen overnight," cautioned Premier Gordon Campbell. "We're all going to be required to change some of our behaviours. We're all going to have to think about what we do, and we're all going to have to be cognizant of the fact that there are impacts from each of our choices."

For British Columbians, it is not enough just to live in the best place on earth. British Columbians are determined to keep it that way.

**Wolf tracks along the Gataga River at sunrise in the Muskwa-Kechika Management Area.**

*Photo John E. Marriott*

# Index

1 2 3 4 5 — 12 11 10 09 08



Produced by Harbour Publishing for BC150 and the Province of British Columbia

Image editing by Vici Johnstone
Production assistant Erin Schopfer
Page, text and map design by Roger Handling
Cover design by Anna Comfort
Cover background image: David Nunuk
Front cover collage, from left to right: snowboarder: Toshi Kowano; logger: Norman Caple photo, City of Vancouver Archives, LGN 727; Nuu-chah-nulth man: Chris Cheadle; Sir James Douglas: Image PDP00090 courtesy of Royal BC Museum, BC Archives; Emily Carr: Image F-01220 courtesy of Royal BC Museum, BC Archives; Inunnguaq: Toshi Kowano; Kermode bear: Ian McAllister; Japanese Canadian woman: Boomer Jerritt
Back cover collage, from left to right: painting of sternwheeler: John Horton; miners: Image B-04823 courtesy of Royal BC Museum, BC Archives; Chief Joseph Gosnell: Gary Fiegehan/*Vancouver Sun*; Indo-Canadian girl: Tom Ryan; Lieutenant Governor David Lam: painting by Cyril Leeper, image courtesy of the Office of the Lieutenant Governor of British Columbia
Front endsheet: Victoria Legislative Buildings: Chris Cheadle
Back endsheet: Totems in Haida Gwaii: Chris Cheadle

Printed in British Columbia 

For sources and more specific information on particular topics see Jean Barman, *The West beyond the West: A History of British Columbia*, 3rd edition (University of Toronto Press, 2007).

**Library and Archives Canada Cataloguing in Publication**

Barman, Jean, 1939-
British Columbia : spirit of the people

"Published ... for BC150 and the Province of British Columbia."—Dust jacket.
ISBN 978-0-7726-5984-2

1. British Columbia - History. 2. British Columbia - Pictorial works. I. British Columbia. BC150 Secretariat. II. British Columbia. III. Title. IV. Title: Spirit of the people.

FC3811.B37 2008 971.1 C2008-960089-4